VENICE BORDERS RE-INTERPRETED

Edited by Paola Favaro,
Anna-Paola Pola and Valentina Tridello

UNSW
SYDNEY
Built Environment

I
U
A
V
Università Iuav
di Venezia

Seidler International Studio Venice
UNSW Built Environment Sydney

Cover:
Campi and Campielli diagrams from Franco Mancuso, *Venezia è una città*, Venezia (2009)
Geometric comparative diagrams from Vladimir Belogolovsky, *Harry Seidler: Lifework,* New York (2014)

Foreword

On Venice and the Biennale
Penelope Seidler: Australian Architect and Director of Sydney-based architectural firm Harry Seidler & Associates.

I am so pleased with the feedback I receive from participants in the Seidler International studio from Venice. My first trip to Venice as a teenager was a treat but it was my second trip when I had completed my architectural degree that I saw the history of architecture spring to life unfolding along the Grand Canal which was thrilling, and every subsequent trip reveals more wonders of this fabulous city.

As a student, we learnt architectural history from the English textbook by Sir Banister Fletcher, it was illustrated by drawings of most of Europe's significant buildings, all gorgeously rendered, the Venetian palazzos were measured and analysed, I learnt more about 'real 'history studying architecture than from formal history teaching! I was amused that Banister Fletcher was not impressed with the sumptuous Santa Maria Della Salute, the baroque scrolls were thought to be decadent and excessive; no doubt an expression of Victorian taste! However, his analysis and descriptions of structure and scale are still worth studying today; we had few photos available to peruse and almost no image projections, just plans and elevations, it was exciting to experience the buildings in three dimensions with texture and couloir in the real!

In Australia, we do not have the experience of living with buildings over 200 years old, not a bad thing, but the grand city of Venice illustrates the integration of buildings through many centuries reflecting their culture and society, they are not static, each century absorbing the contemporary of the era; it is our challenge today to build of our time and to enhance the existing city.

Today Venice is facing major problems, an overload of tourists and a declining population as well as its precipitous tidal and structural dilemmas, it is to be hoped that it does not become a theme park dead city; the results of the UNSW workshops prove that appropriate housing is able to be successfully integrated into the existing Venetian topography, it is still a dynamic live city with modern buildings while still embracing its overpowering heritage.

I confess to being a Venice biennale addict, I have attended every biennale for the last 25 years, both the art and architecture biennales which alternate every year. The architecture biennale is relatively new, and for some years Australia did not participate. It is pleasing that now the Institute of Architects takes it very seriously and calls for submissions every second year. The new pavilion designed by Denton Corker and Marshall is a spectacular building on the canal, an ideal location to mount a meaningful exhibition. During the vernissage streams of visitors' mob through all the pavilions, the game is to entice them to stay more than two minutes to absorb the content; I believe we did this in 2016 with The Pool. The art biennale is quite different, it does not require as much brain work; it is all a question of aesthetics which are judged almost immediately depending on your own personal visual experiences! Whereas the architecture biennale is often confronting as it analyses the problems of the world and often presents pioneering solutions though planning and the built environment; these can be confronting and often question conventional paradigms; I prefer the architecture biennale, it always provides me some fresh insights.

One year I remember that there were panels asking you to access the merits of four cities name Venice, there was Venice Italy, Venice California, Venice Florida and Venice Las Vegas, every city photographed with descriptions and relevant statistics of each, it was up to the viewer to cast a vote, it was quite provocative and forced you to consider the impact of history on contemporary life, I do not know which one came out on top! I have been to three of these Venice's; each of them has many attractions!

I enjoyed a wonderful world of travel with Harry who taught me everything and it does please me that I am able to help today's students experience the benefits of travel and working in inspiring locations.

Penelope Seidler
Sydney

index

Design studio approach: an educated imagination

Paola Favaro, UNSW Built Environment

p. 10 - 17

Harry Seidler's design principles

Paola Favaro, UNSW Built Environment

p. 18 - 25

Sketching the city from history to modernity

UNSW/IUAV students 2015 - 2016

p. 26 - 39

Venice inspiring the world

Valentina Tridello, Università IUAV di Venezia

p. 40 - 43

Venice borders

Enrico Fontanari, Università IUAV di Venezia

p. 44 - 51

The South Front: "La Giudecca"

City in the City (santacroce)
Caterina Barbon, Davide Grandi, Francesco Ceola, Haihong Liu, Matteo Vianello, Yujia Tao

p. 54 - 61

Open Theatre (sanpolo)
Wei Peng, Ruoyu Li, Wei Liu, Yizhan Zhang, Tea Capoia, Chiara Semenzin, Leonardo Peressa

p. 62 - 69

Urban Block (dorsoduro)
Devon Rees, Temyka Belgrove, Anthony Ho, Leslie Xueshen Shen, Janice Quach, Simone Bet, Michela Napolitano

p. 70 - 77

Counterpoint (cannaregio)
Alicia Bell, Nick Bucci, Elise Vanden Dool, Thida Sachathep, Francesca Perer, Silvia Pellizzon

p. 78 - 85

City of Corridors and Campi (sanmarco)
Janice Yeung Yan Xie, Piera Favaretto, Alice Gruarin, Yushan Yue, Siyi Huang

p. 86 - 93

Influx (castello)
Chelsea Sheriden, Paige Zhang, Jacqueline Oliver, Taya Brooks, Michelangelo Mezzocolli, Samereh Nouri, Aghjeh Kandi

p. 94 - 103

The North Front:
"Fondamenta Nuove"

I U A V
Università Iuav di Venezia

DIPARTIMENTO
DI CULTURE DEL PROGETTO

UNIVERSITY OF NEW
SOUTH WALES - UNSW
SIDNEY

SEIDLER INTERNATIONAL VENICE STUDIO-SIVS

workshop

docenti
Enrico Fontanari, Iuav
Paola Favaro, UNSW
James Weirick, UNSW

tutor
Valentina Tridello, Iuav

aperto alle Lauree Magistrali in architettura
di tutti i dipartimenti - **4 crediti tipologia D**
info e iscrizioni: henry@iuav.it - www.iuav.it

**22.11>2.12.2016
Ca' Tron
Aula B1**

Laguna North
Yuchen Xia, Bowen Li, Dimitri Azzarà, Luca Emilio Longo
p. 104 - 111

Santa Giustina Proposal (sanpolo)
Joanne Ly, Erin Arthur, Man Hin Ma, Sally Yuen, Miriam Elia, Caterina Dubini, Federico Tommasoni
p. 112 - 119

Nexus (dorsoduro)
Lauren Rutstein, Sarah MacDonald, Carlos Veas, Diana Yang, Yunjing Guan, Timis Maria, Grippo Alessia
p. 120 - 127

Cultural Revival (san polo)
Tina Kan, Yi Ren, Yan Man Tong, Sik Wai Tam, Laura Andretta, Valentina Fracca
p. 128 - 135

Campo Zero (cannaregio)
Laura Ng, Amy McNicol, Selma Tursunovic, Sadina Tursunovic, Sobia Ameen, Bonetto Anna, Zudich Eleonora
p. 136 - 143

Interlace (san marco)
Madeleine Stocker, Fera Rexhina, Amandeep Kaur, Kyar NyoYin, Claudia Borgogno, Nee Shuang Heng
p. 144 - 151

Connections (castello)
Hai Lan Wang, Laure Pieren, Caterina Carpenè, Lan Anh Doh, Angel Miu, Giulio Grienti, Manasi Kundap
p. 152 - 161

Design studio approach:
An educated imagination
Paola Favaro, UNSW Built Environment

Inspired by Harry Seidler design approach and funded by the architect and benefactor Penelope Seidler with the Seidler Architectural Foundation, the Seidler International Studio took place in 2015 and 2016 as a collaboration between the UNSW Sydney Built Environment and IUAV University of Venice.

The design studio proposed the urban and architectural transformation of the southern edge of Venice on La Giudecca Island in 2015 and of the northern edge of Venice along the Castello Sestiere (neighbour) in 2016.

A robust design framework was activated by cultivating in the students an 'educated imagination' through the integration of research, critical thinking, field work study and a structured system of assessment tasks. In order to develop an appropriate design proposal it was necessary to appreciate a historical city like Venice with its traditional architecture and urban system in relation to its current social and political situations.

Harry Seidler's words assisted the students as a framework for their appreciation, analysis and conceptual /organizing strategy:

After some years, circumnavigating of the globe started with ever increasing frequency – to experience the most celebrated ancient and current architecture in Europe, Asia and America. With frequent stops in Rome to consult with the engineer Pier Luigi Nervi on my concrete structures, I first experienced the impact of historic architecture in any depth. Developing what I call a passive appreciation and respect for the great building achievements of the past – I saw this as a simultaneous active love and dedication to developing an appropriate architecture, expressive of the artistic and technological impacts in building today. One can appreciate traditional architecture in relation to its period, the given circumstances of man's artistic aspirations, technical means and the social political conditions of the time, as against the involved, active enthusiasm evoked by the masterpieces of the time in which one builds.[1]

During his many travels around the world to follow his international projects, Seidler developed a love for photography, which he used to document his visits to examples of what he considered the most beautiful architecture achieved throughout time. His book The Grand Tour is an extraordinary resource, with the camera capturing the architects' visual and spatial imagination and constructional logic involved in the realization of the buildings. Seidler's design principles and photographic records, collected while travelling, informed the students' critical analysis and documentation of a number of selected architecture projects as well as their own design project.

By thoroughly investigating the historical urban system and urban typologies of Venice, as well as specific historical and current architectural precedents, students questioned aspects of architecture, urban forms and interior spaces exploring the opportunity to redevelop a series of existing sites along the southern and northern edges of Venice - from the outside to the inside.

The first activity was thus, focussed on an appreciation of the place of Venice through the morphological analysis of a typical insula of the historic centre of Venice.

So what lesson could the students draw from the insula's urban morphology with its land system (campo, campiello, calle, ruga, ramo, fondamenta) and water system (canal, river or lagoon)? How did the open space of the campo, its form and function in constant dialogue with the architecture of its public and commercial buildings, its private habitations and religious buildings work? Does the campo still hold urban and architectural elements, which can be valid today? The study of the insula's urban form offered the students the cultural awareness of Venice as a historical and modern city, appreciating Le Corbusier's 1935 statement "Venice is my model for every city of the future".

Each group was assigned one insula and one campo from the six sestieri: Santa Croce, Dorsoduro, San Polo, Cannaregio, San Marco and Castello.

Students responded to this first activity through a series of individual hand drawings to include the expertise of each discipline: the overall planning organization, the architectural volume and spatial ambiance, the intimate interior spaces of specific public or religious buildings, commercial and private habitation and their relationship with the constructed urban landscape of the campo.

Analysis of Venice as a modern city: walking through Venice with an architect's eye.

By questioning the contemporary projects within each individual sestiere, students were asked to consider them through Seidler's design approach. Seidler embraced clear design principles based on spatial imagination and technological innovation coupled with constructional logic, which he believed could achieve a higher level of design, especially if they were guided by influential modernist artists, architects and engineers.

Did the selected project explore clear design principles? Was the selected project based on a coherent ideology embracing and fusing "visual and spatial imagination, technological integration and constructional logic"? Based in the UNSW/IUAV interdisciplinary studio, did the selected project explore the integration of the four disciplines: planning, architecture, interior architecture and landscape architecture? Did the planning organization lead to a convincing solution in terms of the relation between the ground floor from the outside to the inside spaces, the approach to the building, the entrance and the circulation through the building? What could students draw from the analysis of the selected examples?

The discussion based on research, analysis and the representation of selected precedents, required students to argue (compare and contrast) issues relevant to the site project/context not merely their personal preferences. The intent was for specific activities connected to the urban project to stimulate a broad awareness of planning organization, architectural volumes, landscape architecture and interior spaces. Most importantly, students were asked to question how the selected precedents were useful for their group site and their group brief.

By visiting a series of contemporary buildings realised recently in each sestiere, the International studio offered the students the opportunity to discover how Venice is a modern city. In Sestiere Santa Croce the 2013 Cittadella della Giustizia, (Court of Justice) by Cappai Mainardis; the new infrastructure of Francesco Cocco's People Mover Infrastructure (2010) and the controversial Ponte della Costituzione (Constitution Bridge) (2008) by Santiago Calatrava revealed from a close distance how buildings and infrastructure were inserted into the Piazzale Roma surroundings. While in Sestiere Dorsoduro, students discovered how apparently historical buildings have been completely transformed on the inside by a clever new planning configuration and material additions. Tadao Ando's 2009 Punta Della Dogana (Custom House), Vittorio De Feo's 2006 Santa Marta Church and Renzo Piano's 2009 Fondazione Vedova alle Zattere proved the case.

New residential and affordable housing projects realised outside the predictable touristic paths enabled the students to analyse in La Giudecca island how Carlo Aymonino's, Aldo Ross's and Alvaro Siza's Residenze a Campo di Marte (2002-2009) and Cino Zucchi Ex Junghans, (1997-2003) interpreted the urban typology of the campo with its private and public buildings.

In Sestiere Cannaregio, students visited David Chipperfield's San Michele island cemetery (2007-current); Vittorio Gregotti's Ex Saffa housing complex (1985-2001). While in Sestiere San Marco students visited Pier Luigi Nervi's Palazzo Nervi Scattolin, Cassa di Risparmio (1970) and Tadao Ando's Teatrino Grassi in Campo San Samuele, (Grassi Theatre) (2013). At last in Sestiere Castello within the Arsenale area of the historical shipyard from the Renaissance period, Alberto Cecchetto intervened with the new CNR-ISMAR laboratories (2008-2009) and Francesco Magnani with his Torre di Porta Nuova project (2011).

A special acknowledgment was given to Carlo Scarpa's projects: in particular to his 1963 Fondazione Querini Stampalia with additions by Mario Botta (2013) and his Olivetti shop in Piazza San Marco.

Biennale of Art and Architecture

A significant component of the Seidler International Design Studio was to expose students to aspects of international contemporary art, architecture and urban design, experienced by visiting the 2015 Venice Biennale of Art and the 2016 Venice Biennale of Architecture, titled 'Reporting from the Front,' aptly curated by Chilean architect and social activist Alexandro Aravena at the Giardini and Arsenale. Giardini is an area located on the eastern part of the island, historically textured by orchards and gardens (giardini), which hosts a series of international pavilions built specifically for the recurring event of the Biennale of Art and Architecture.

For over a century, all the pavilions which draw millions of visitors from across the globe have been used as exalted, contemplative areas for viewing unique and important works of art and architecture. Clearly, the pavilion for showing art and architecture installations provides visitors with a ceremonial experience: they communicate the values and beliefs of the architects who designed them, as well as the artists and architects whose works are shown in them. Yet the architectural/structural, elements/frameworks of these pavilions often seem to blur the boundary between art and architecture, leading us to ask whether the architecture of the pavilion is used as a container of art, or whether its architectural form, the container itself, should be interpreted as art.

The various architectural pavilions all reveal the diverse directions that various individual architects have taken within the time frame of approximately 120 years.[2] During this period, the *Giardini* area has hosted the Biennale of Arts and the Biennale of Architecture within a series of international pavilions designed by well-known international architects. In 1922, the design of the Spanish pavilion encouraged the construction of other new innovative international pavilions including Carlo Scarpa's Venezuelan Pavilion, (1954) Alvar Aalto's Finnish Pavilion (1955), Sverre Fehn's Nordic Countries Pavilion (1962) and more recently Philip Cox's Australian Pavilion (1988) and Franco Mancuso's Korean Pavilion (2004). In such exhibition spaces, each country's cultural values and ideals have been represented through the various architectures of the pavilions. Historically, the practice of designing architectural pavilions as containers for art, usually built for recurring events such as World Fairs or other various Expos can, in a sense be seen as part of a cyclical pattern where time continues to flow and move from one event to the next, from one place, city, country, continent to the next. Yet by contrast, the pavilions of Venice have been purpose-built within the same place, the *Giardini*, for the recurring event of the Venice Biennale, thus embodying a more static or constant presence within the urban fabric of a specific city/place.

Denton Corker Marshall's Australian Pavilion opened in May 2015 for the Biennale of Arts. It replaced the temporary pavilion of Philip Cox (1988) with a confrontational and controversial cube - black outside and white inside, defined in a journal article penned by Melbourne architect Robert Grace as '…a clever architecture response to the commissioner's suspicion of architecture, his concern about the architecture dominating the art…' [3]

For the Australian students it was important to visit the Australian Pavilion in 2015 to engage with the art exhibition by Fiona Hall and with the architectural exhibition "The Pool" by Aileen Sage in 2016. While in Fiona Hall's installation the Pavilion was all covered up including the window on the canal, for "The Pool" the curators kept the window open to invite a dialogue between their project about water and this unique city of water. Interestingly, for the UNSW students it was a great discovery and opportunity to acknowledge the success of Amelia Halliday, a graduate from the School of Architecture at UNSW, who together with Isabelle Toland, was one of the creative directors behind Aileen Sage's winning scheme.

In 2015 a visit to the *Proportio* exhibition held in Palazzo Fortuny inspired the students to revisit antiquity and the Roman architecture through Vitruvian principles of *Firmitas, Utilitas* and *Venustas* and admire the rules of proportions including the Golden Section, also visible in Palladio's churches such as San Giorgio Maggiore and Redentore.

The project

Based on the critique of the current and increasing monofunctional tourist economy, the two interdisciplinary design proposals on the southern and northern edges of Venice were advocates for good architecture and urban transformation. The intent was to develop a diverse and mixed-use neighbourhood while maintaining a reasonable number of Venetian residents, by increasing the number of residential units and affordable housing, by providing flexible uses of public spaces and by adapting unutilized, historic, industrial buildings for public facilities.

There is a growing recognition within the built environment that an interdisciplinary design approach will develop a better vision for our cities. The Seidler International Studio provided an opportunity for students to investigate a historical city with a unique urban system, where the individual buildings have been planned and constructed together with the urban space. Venice's urban system proved to be aligned with Seidler's own design approach, in which architecture along with planning and urban design work to achieve a t*otal environment.*

In May 1967, Seidler was invited in Brisbane to speak at the annual convention of the Australian Architectural Student Association. Responding to the convention's theme "City Synthesis", Seidler gave a memorable speech where he suggested: "Everyone is complaining about the lack of planning and the ugliness of cities ... Unfortunately, no-one has ever seen or experienced a really good city, a city which takes full advantage of today's better technology and design planning. A city planned so everybody could walk to work in less time than it takes to get there by car or subway ... I have the ambition in my life, and I have set about this ever since I started out, not to build buildings, but to build if not cities total environments." [4]

In the same year Seidler's first tower, Australia Square, (1961-1967) opened in Sydney. What Seidler achieved with Australia Square and in the following years with MLC Centre (1971-1977), Grosvenor Place (1982-1988), Capita Centre (1984-1989) and the Cove Apartments (2003-2004), his five Sydney Towers, was arguably the design of total environments still valid today as it was 50 year ago.

To achieve total environments, Seidler as a modernist architect, sought out successful architects, artists, planners, landscape architects and engineers for inspiration and collaboration. Learning from Seidler's inclusive collaborative design, this studio promoted interdisciplinary learning and a multidisciplinary approach to design.

Students were engaged with the relevant concerns and the vision for the future of Venice, learning to appreciate it as a model for a modern city of the future addressing contemporary problems of the built environment.

Venice Borders adopted clear design principles derived from an in-depth reading of Venice's urban system and its residential and public urban typologies. Along with the historical analysis students analysed Venice's modernist and contemporary projects keeping in mind Harry Seidler's design principles, while being exposed to the Biennale of Art and Architecture.

The daily studio critical sessions asked the students to answer a series of questions: What lessons did the students learn from the historical analysis of Venice's urban form and urban typologies? What design principles were they able to discover through the analysis of Venice's contemporary projects?

To what extent did the visit to the Biennale of Art, the Giardini pavilions and the artists' installations influence their planning spatial imagination?

These questions assisted the students in their design process by adopting a critical approach to the interpretation of the project site and the context within the Giudecca island on the southern border of Venice and Castello Sestiere on the northern border of Venice.

The urban space of the *campo* with the architecture of the surrounding volumes and interior spaces in constant dialogue with the overall landscape of the lagoon edges, guided their projects without falling into the two extremes of being too careful and conservative or too bold and iconic.

Ultimately, it was a strong conviction of this studio that an elegant solution with a clear design framework that goes beyond the interpretation of the brief, site and context to embrace a modern language, will always stand its time when placed in a specific site and context.

Vladimir Belogolovsky suggested in his recent publication, *Harry Seidler LifeWork*:

> *Today Architects and students all over the world dig through the latest publications and visit the newest buildings in search for new design ideas. The work of Harry Seidler directs them to find inspiration in many original sources and to explore numerous possibilities in their interpretations to address their own time and place.*[5]

From the vantage point of the present, which seems to privilege what has been ironically called 'decorated sheds', how might we still understand, appreciate and learn from Seidler's design values the potential of the modernist period while enthusing the students with the principles of modern architecture? The following proposition by Seidler seemed to respond to this question:

> *To sum up, I would say that these tendencies shown are not necessarily evident to most people. People tend to not want formulas, not want to recognise criteria that should guide us but in my view unless there are criteria, unless there is consensus about that which does influence and tantalize the eye in our age it would be very difficult for us to find and explore those directions that have proven, at least for half, if not three quarters, of a century to be considered beautiful, satisfying and worthy of pursuit into the future.*[6]

Thus, through these words bearing both a step toward the past and a vision toward the future, a series of criteria have guided the students in the design of a sequence of informed and thoughtful projects re-interpreting the borders of south and north of Venice.

[1] Harry Seidler, *The Grand Tour: Travelling the World with an Architect's Eye*, 2003.

[2] Marco Mulazzani, *I Padiglioni della Biennale di Venezia 1887-1988*, Venezia: Edizioni La Biennale di Venezia, 1988. Introduzione pp.7-14. From 1887 the neoclassical winning design of Raimondo d'Aronco for the façade of the Italian pavilion (subsequently re-designed by Guido Cirilli in 1914, Duilio Torres in 1932 and Carlo Scarpa in 1968) to the nationalistic sentiments visible in the 1934 Greek and 1938 German pavilions while strong Palladian overtones are visible in the 1909 British and 1930 American pavilions.

[3] Robert Grace, *Cultural embassy, Australian Pavilion, Venice*, in ARCHITECTUREAU, 15 October 2015, http://architectureau.com/articles/australian-pavilion-venice/

[4] John Davis, Students investigate City Synthesis – Architecture Today, July 1967

[5] Vladimir Belogolovsky, Harry Seidler LifeWork, Rizzoli, (2014): p.11

[6] Lecture One Interaction: Architecture and the Visual Arts, p.9. "Harry Seidler Lectures on Architecture (1980). The videotaped version of the six lectures and their transcriptions are available on the UNSW Built Environment website.

Harry Seidler's design principles
Paola Favaro, UNSW Built Environment

In 2015 and 2016 Seidler International Studios have been influenced by the Austrian-born Sydney architect Harry Seidler (Vienna 1923-Sydney 2006).

Seidler is considered one of Australia's foremost architects. His work includes award winning single houses built within the spectacular Sydney harbor, public and private buildings within Sydney Civic Centre and a great variety of projects built around Australia and the world including the Australian Embassy in Paris (1973-77) and the Neue Donau Social Estate (1999-2002) in his home-town Vienna.

Seidler's design principles with art, architecture and technology merging together, are informed by his European and American architecture education and work experience, his formal exposure to the Bauhaus pedagogy as a student and a recent graduate with international architects like Walter Gropius and Marcel Breuer and by the encounter with the Italian engineer Pier Luigi Nervi (1891-1979). With Nervi, Seidler collaborated to the design and construction of Australia Square (1961-1967) and the MLC Centre (1971-1977) both realized in Sydney.

Seidler embraced two principles: spatial imagination and technological innovation coupled with constructional logic, that he believed could achieve a higher level of design, especially if they were guided by influential modernist artists, architects and engineers. Thus, his design approach was to strive for spatial imagination, to be achieved through visual education, for constructional logic, which could be learned by understanding the technological innovation during the modernist period.

In accordance, in the first instance, *spatial imagination*, he was influenced by the work of painters and sculptors from the modernist period and by the work of Italian and German architects from the baroque era (1650–1750), exploring the way they used art and architecture in the context of space.

By borrowing specific visual and geometric propositions, such as *channeling of vistas, asymmetry, dematerialization of solidity and transparency,* as well as the specific compositional design elements of *geometry, movement, access, structure, concave and convex*, Seidler was searching for successful architectural projects realized by modernist and contemporary architects.

In the second instance, in the case of *constructional logic*, Seidler revisited the exemplary work of the Swiss engineer Robert Maillart (1872–1940) and the Italian engineer from Rome Pier Luigi Nervi (1891–1979). With Nervi, Seidler collaborated in the design and construction of Australia Square (1962–67) and the MLC Centre (1971–77). Interestingly, we can find a connection between Pier Luigi Nervi and Seidler also in Venice. The invitation to the students was to visit the bank Cassa di Risparmio di Venezia (1970-1972), also called Palazzo Nervi, between Campo San Luca

Harry Seidler in his studio, Killara House, Sydney.
Courtesy of Harry Seidler & Associates Archive.

and Campo Manin designed by engineer Nervi in collaboration with the Venetian architect Angelo Scattolin. In their analysis, students appreciated how Nervi was able to interpret the typical Venetian architectural elements, geometry and proportions to re-invent a modernist palazzo through a sensitive and innovative spatial, constructional and material design.

It was through the solid imagination of an engineer like Nervi that Seidler addressed creatively his approach to structural problems and their interaction with the architectural forms. The synthesis of these two themes, with technology as counterpoint to art, can be read as the culmination of an *organizational design framework*.

One has to remember that new technologies and new materials introduced a freedom in the design and realization of certain buildings, because load-bearing walls were already obsolete by the end of the 1930s.

So, what did Seidler learn from his main influences, from the lessons he learned as a loyal disciple, not only of Walter Gropius and Marcel Breuer, but also of the other Bauhaus émigrés in the United States? The lessons from the modernist masters can be seen in the planning composition of his numerous projects, beginning with the Rose Seidler House (1949) and his own house in Killara (1966). The constructional logic as organizational design framework is visible in both houses but using different construction techniques, as pointed out by art and architecture historian Barry Bergdoll:

"But I think most historians would see the big shift there in the expression from this very lightweight engineering timber structure cantilevered off the ground [Rose Seidler House] to a structure with a great dependence on reinforced concrete [Killara House]."[1]

As a point of interest, Penelope and Harry's house in Killara was designed after Harry encountered Nervi. One can argue that Seidler's play of cantilevered concrete volumes and the dialogue of solids and voids was Seidler's own interpretation of Nervi's influential engineering and aesthetic use of concrete.

In Sydney, Seidler explored the dematerialization of space and mass, exploding the typical normal rooms of a house into a continuum of spaces, freestanding planes, and cantilevered floor slab. For Seidler, designing continuous, dematerialized spaces created radical new possibilities. Thus, as the legacy of the modernist period, dematerialized spaces should be respected, re-evaluated, and relayed to students.

Seidler's belief that constructional logic underpins successful design is evident in his own work including the Thredbo Ski Lodge (1962), the Hong Kong Club (1980–84), and the Australian Embassy in Paris (1973–77). Thus, in these projects the organizational design framework was reinforced by a well-chosen structural theme whose impact was central to further design decisions and material selection.

To reinforce this argument one has only to visit Seidler's Trade Group Offices (later renamed the Edmund Barton Building), in Canberra, and the MLC Centre in Sydney. These two projects were designed to use only three industrially produced concrete structural components:

1. a long span beam that works also as a façade element (with continuous, recessed windows between them);
2. a precast column;
3. a floor plank connected by pre-stressing wires to produce unity.[2]

Ideas around the impact of contemporary construction techniques (that we felt would be embraced by Seidler if he were practicing today) included the use of advanced 'design- make' computational technology to continue his theme of 'pre-fabrication' to deliver innovative architectural form with economy."[3]

In both the Trade Group Office and the MLC Centre, the constructional logic was a system of repetitive elements. In questioning what Seidler would do now, we can probably say that today, the difference is that prefabrication using advanced computational technologies does not require the same level of repetition as in the Seidler era. Mass customization of building components is now available, creating more opportunity for the exploration of spatial and sculptural ideas that can be produced effectively and economically, in accordance with one of Seidler's principles." [4]

In terms of visual and spatial imagination, Seidler's belief on the role and interaction of architecture with art is well expressed here: "The visual arts of our time have had as much to do with the visual language that has come to make up Modern Architecture." He further suggested: "The related community of principles aims and results in all the visual arts, evaluating the language of space, of visual tensions and generally showing what our eyes respond to positively, and just what the common denominators in our language of vision are today."[5]

Seidler always drew for his visual and spatial imagination from the exemplary work of cubist painters, and inter alia, the Bauhaus artists Joseph Albers (1888-1976), László Moholy-Nagy (1895–1946), and Johannes Itten (1888-1967). Their art defies time and space through their three dimensional compositions.

In a similar way, Seidler's fascination for the baroque architecture was intended as vehicle to develop creativity: "... a survey of a significant period in history, [baroque] which has been called the last great creative period prior to our own, illustrating and seeing the similarity of consequential thought, then and now, of system-geometry, spatial interplay and flair for dramatization."[6]

For Seidler, the Italian architect Francesco Borromini and his church Sant' Ivo alla Sapienza was one of the most celebrated and influential example of baroque architecture. In Sant' Ivo, the axial approach of the Renaissance period is lost for a spatial imagination achieved through interior and exterior concave and convex forms that intertwine with each other in alternate bays and continue to the dome above.

So perhaps a plausible question is: to what extent the baroque architecture is visible in Seidler's use of geometry, construction innovation and technological integration? And to what extent the lessons of the baroque but most importantly of the modernist architecture has survived the time?

Seidler used to blame local architects for dismissing the lessons of modern architecture, stating:

"I believe it is important to reiterate some of the creative origins, and where and what are the principles of modern architecture, where they have their roots and where are they going and, above all, where should we go."[7]

As a modernist architect, Seidler sought out successful artists, architects, and engineers for inspiration and collaboration suggesting that what is called twentieth-century modern architecture is built upon "a synthesis of all the concerns of painters, sculptors, technicians, engineers."[8]

Seidler speaks of this synthesis as "discernable criteria, which make up the principles of modern architecture recognizable in different ways in different parts of the word." In this lecture, he clarifies his belief in an architectural language that uses both influences from art and technology to foster creativity.

Seidler asks the rhetorical question, "What, now, are the principles?" In response, he links spatial imagination and constructional logic, and how, for him, these two complementary aspects merge to realize the aesthetics of the modern architecture of the twentieth century.

Introducing Seidler's design principles in the International Design Studios, the intention was to adopt his coherent design approach by fusing visual and spatial imagination, technological integration and constructional logic. We can say that the work produced by the students in developing the south border of La Giudecca Island in 2015 and the north border of Castello in 2016 were influenced by Seidler's theoretical reflections on the Bauhaus lessons on visual education and spatial imagination and by the structural innovations of an engineer like Nervi. Interestingly, as already suggested, students were able to visit Palazzo Nervi in Campo Manin in Venice and appreciate Nervi's own aesthetic qualities and design framework.

Questioning what would Seidler do today?

By drawing directly on Seidler's design approach, the aim was to introduce students not only to his thought, but also to the world from which he came. Seidler's design principles, which he adopted during his career have been sustained from the first project for Rose Seidler house in the 1950s to one of the last projects of the Cove Apartments and the Ian Thorpe Swimming Pool in Ultimo, Sydney fifty years later.

In his writing and professional work, Seidler promoted the belief that the "essence of modern architecture is based on a coherent ideology embracing and fusing spatial imagination, technological integration and constructional logic." My own position, which underpins this "updating" in Seidler International studio in Venice, is that there is currently a lack in the realm of academics and among practitioners of such a coherent ideology.

In this vacuum, project "decorations" accumulate, rather than signs of a clear and articulated system of principles. Australian architectural historian Philip Drew ends *Two Towers* with an argument that substantiates this position.

Referring to Australia Square and the MLC Centre, both designed before 1980, Drew wrote, "The towers embody important technical advances and demonstrate a skill in handling form, which is only possible where the architect is clear in his own mind about the proper tasks of architecture." [9]

It is widely accepted that Seidler's architecture has affected the tone of the civic centre of Sydney in a positive sense. Visiting Seidler's city towers, and passing through their expressive external volumes into their animated interior spaces, one experiences what Seidler advocated in his 1964 article "Architecture Appropriate to Australia":

"Planes opposing each other in space . . . solid opposed by void, cold colour against warm, curve against straight line and above all in Australia's climate, sunlight against shadow." [10]

Harry Seidler and his architecture from the exhibition *Painting Toward Architecture* curated by Vladimir Belogolovsky, Sydney (2014).

[1] Harry Seidler, *Six Lectures*, filmed and produced by Closed Circuit Television UNSW, 10 April-27 June 1980. The videotaped version of the six lectures and their transcriptions are available on the UNSW Built Environment website. Barry Bergdoll's response to lecture 6 at the Lunch time lecture at the Faculty of the Built Environment, UNSW, 2014.

[2] "Harry Seidler Lectures on Architecture (1980)," lecture 3, "Consequence of Design and Detail," transcript, p. 5.

[3] Notes by Alec Tzannes for his introduction to lecture 3, Lunch Time lecture at the Faculty of the Built Environment, 4 September 2014, UNSW.

[4] Notes by Alec Tzannes for his introduction to lecture 3, Lunch Time lecture at the Faculty of the Built Environment, 4 September 2014, UNSW.

[5] Ibid., lecture 1, "Interaction: Architecture and the Visual Arts," transcript, p. 3.

[6] Ibid., lecture 2, "Form Relations in Baroque and Modern Architecture, Part 1," transcript, p. 5.

[7] "Harry Seidler Lectures on Architecture (1980)," lecture 5, "Habitat: Its Detail and Totality," transcript, p. 2.

[8] "Harry Seidler Lectures on Architecture (1980)," lecture 6, "Principles in the Mainstream of Modern Architecture," transcript, p. 5.

[9] Philip Drew, *Two Towers. Harry Seidler: Australia Square, M.L.C. Centre*, (Sydney: Horwitz Grahame Books, 1980), p.11.

[10] Harry Seidler, "Architecture Appropriate to Australia," *Architecture Today*, August 1964, p.15.

View of Sydney Harbour with MLC Center (1978).
Courtesy of Harry Seidler & Associate Archive.

Sketching the city

Sestiere Santa Croce: Cappai Mainardis, Cittadella della Giustizia (Court of Justice)(2013); Francesco Cocco, People Mover Infrastructure (2010); Santiago Calatrava, Ponte della Costituzione (Constitution Bridge) (2008);

Sestiere Dorsoduro: Tadao Ando, Punta Della Dogana (Custom House) Zattere (2007-2009): Vittorio De Feo, Santa Marta Church (2006), Renzo Piano, Fondazione Vedova alle Zattere (2009)

Sestiere San Polo: Aldo Aymonino, Aldo Rossi, Alvaro Siza, Residenze a Campo di Marte, Giudecca Island (2002-2009), Cino Zucchi Ex Junghans, Giudecca Island, (1997-2003)

Sestiere Cannaregio: David Chipperfield, San Michele island cemetery (2007-current); Vittorio Gregotti, Ex Saffa housing complex (1985-2001)

Sestiere San Marco: Pier Luigi Nervi, Palazzo Nervi Scattolin, Cassa di Risparmio (1970) [http://progettocultura.intesasanpaolo.com/it/visita/palazzi-storici/palazzo-nervi-scattolin]; Tadao Ando, Teatrino Grassi, Campo San Samuele, (Grassi Theatre) (2013)

Sestiere Castello: Alberto Cecchetto, new CNR-ISMAR laboratories, Arsenale (2008-2009); Francesco Magnani, Torre di Porta Nuova, Arsenale (2011); Carlo Scarpa (1963) + Mario Botta (2013) Fondazione Querini Stampalia.

from history to modernity
UNSW/IUAV students 2015 - 2016

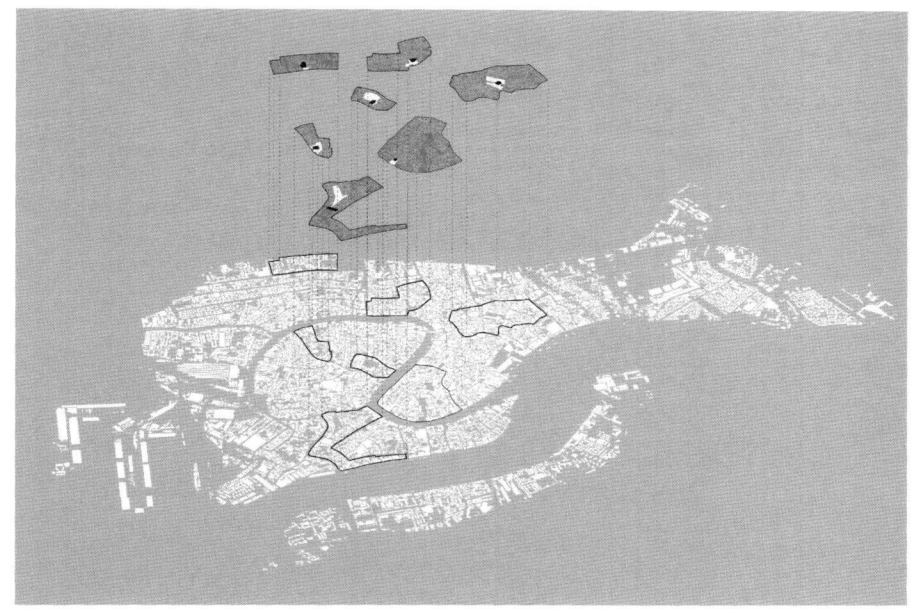

Santa croce

COMPARATIVE STUDY.
   OLD & NEW.

COMPARISONS
- BRIDGE
- NARROW / WIDE - FRAMED VIEWS.
- LACK OF SQUARE IN NEW
- RELATIONSHIP TO WATER
- ALTERATIONS VS BRAND NEW CONSTRUCT.
- RELIGIOUS - SOCIAL AREAS
- TRANSPORT
- FRAMT

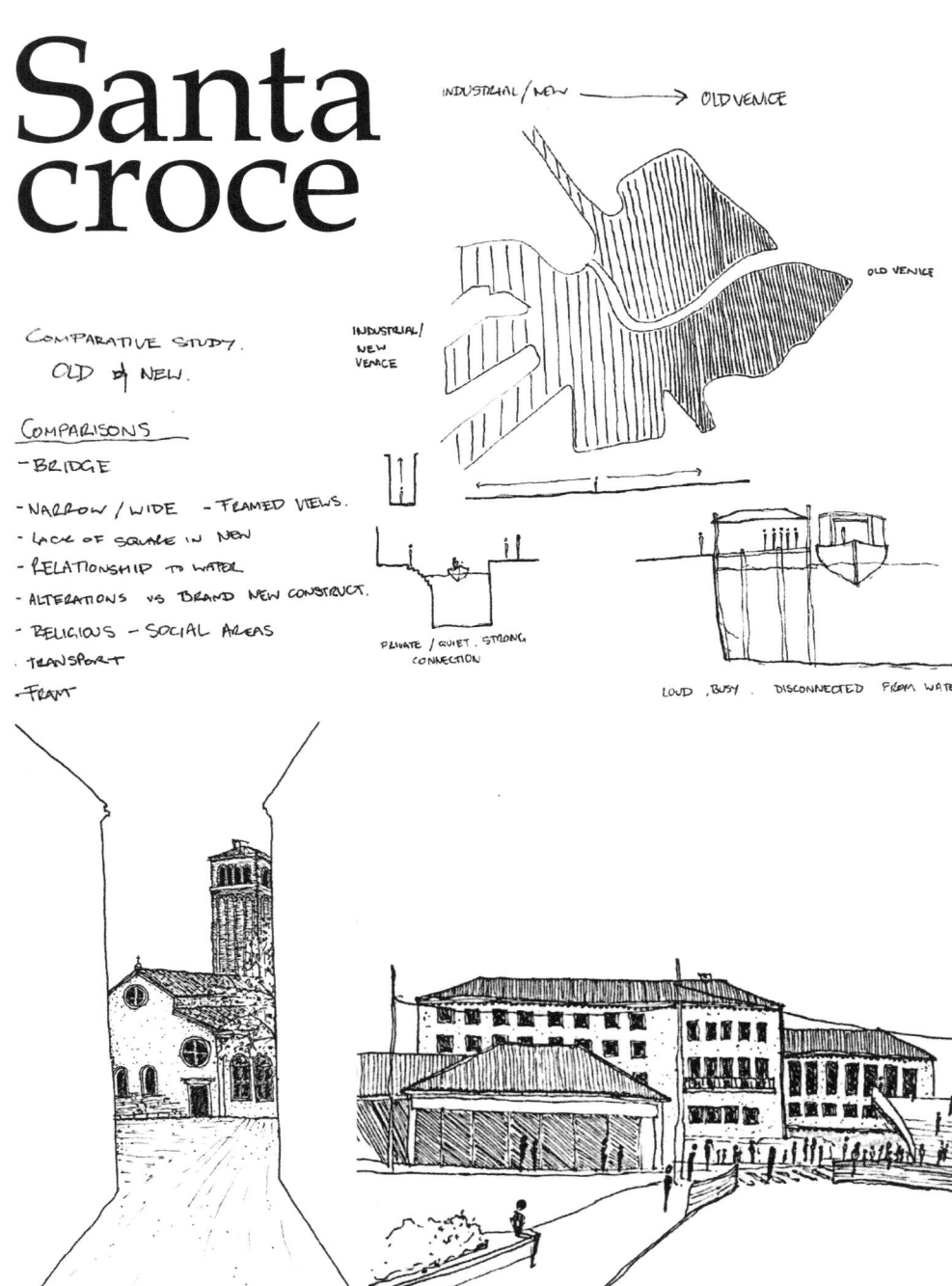

NEW STYLE BUILDINGS   OLD VENICE BUILDING STYLES

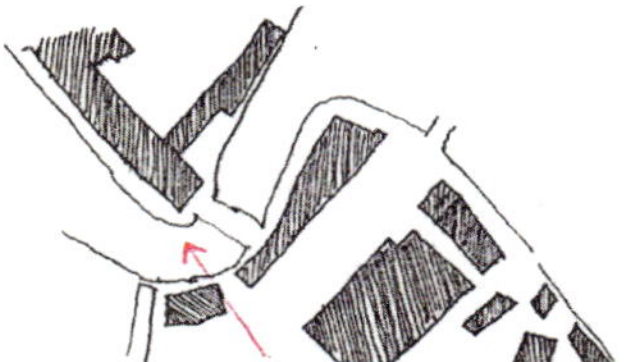

Dorsoduro

DORSODURO LOCATION PLAN

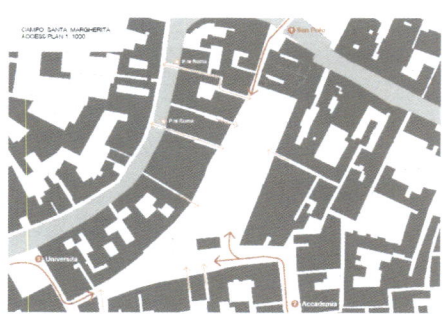

CAMPO SANTA MARGHERITA ACCESS PLAN 1:1000

CAMPO SANTA MARGHERITA STREET ELEVATION

Residential

Commercial

CAMPO SANTA MARGHERITA PROGRAM LAYOUT 1:1000

LEGEND
- Church
- Former police station
- Residential
- Educational
- Commercial
- Canals

DERILICT HISTORICAL WELL

CIVIC BUILDING - FORMER POLICE STATION

CHURCH OF SANTA MARTA

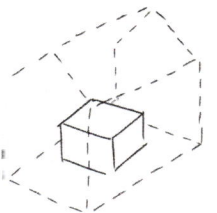

CIRCULATION
By separating the insertion from the original building, the structure becomes almost sculptural, allowing people to circulate around and through the addition.

REVERENCE
The new architecture is completely separate from the historic masonry shell which conveys a reverence towards the original building. The insertion did not alter the structure, but rather brought new life to the derelict site.

FONDAZIONE VEDOVA

Preserving and revealing the old surfaces and elements of the original building

Renzo Piano's insertion and new elements

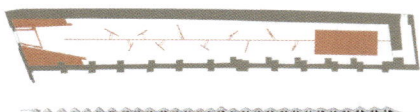

TRANSITION
The floor level has been continued from the exterior to the interior to allow for an eased transition through the thresholds.

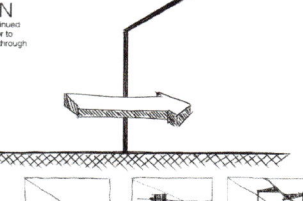

Unconventional way of displaying paintings: Floating in the air exploring movement and flexible-mechanical system

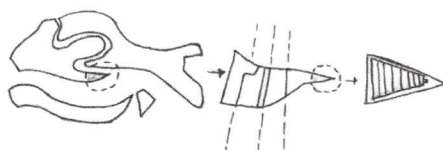
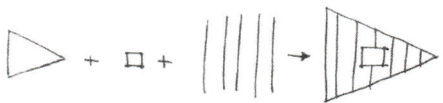

TRIANGLE
A direct reference to the shape of the end

CUBE
concrete cube in the middle the triangle

LINE
series of parallel walls that divided the

PUNTA DELLA DOGANA: GEOMETRY
_Genuis Loci, the spirit of the space
_Simplistic geometric form
_Conservation of history and essenceof the space

COMMERCIAL - GROUND | RESIDENTIAL - ABOVE

MARKET STALLS

San Polo

Giudecca

Giudecca is made up of 8 small islands that are interconnected by a number of bridges as well as a long fondamenta along it's homonymous canal. The diagram shows the main circulation of the island.

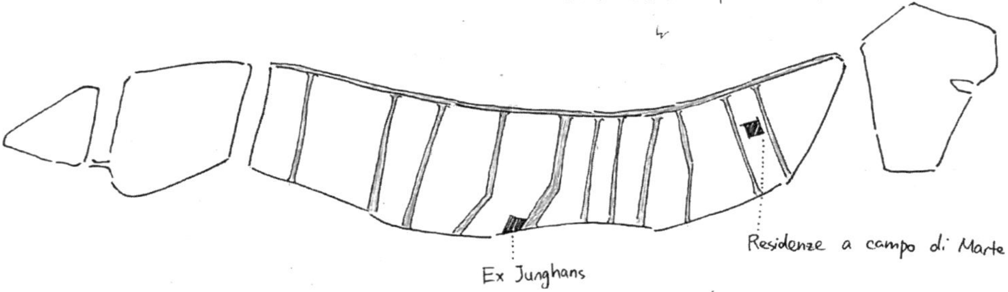

Ex Junghans

Residenze a campo di Marte

Aldo Rossi

Carlo Aymonino

Alvaro Siza

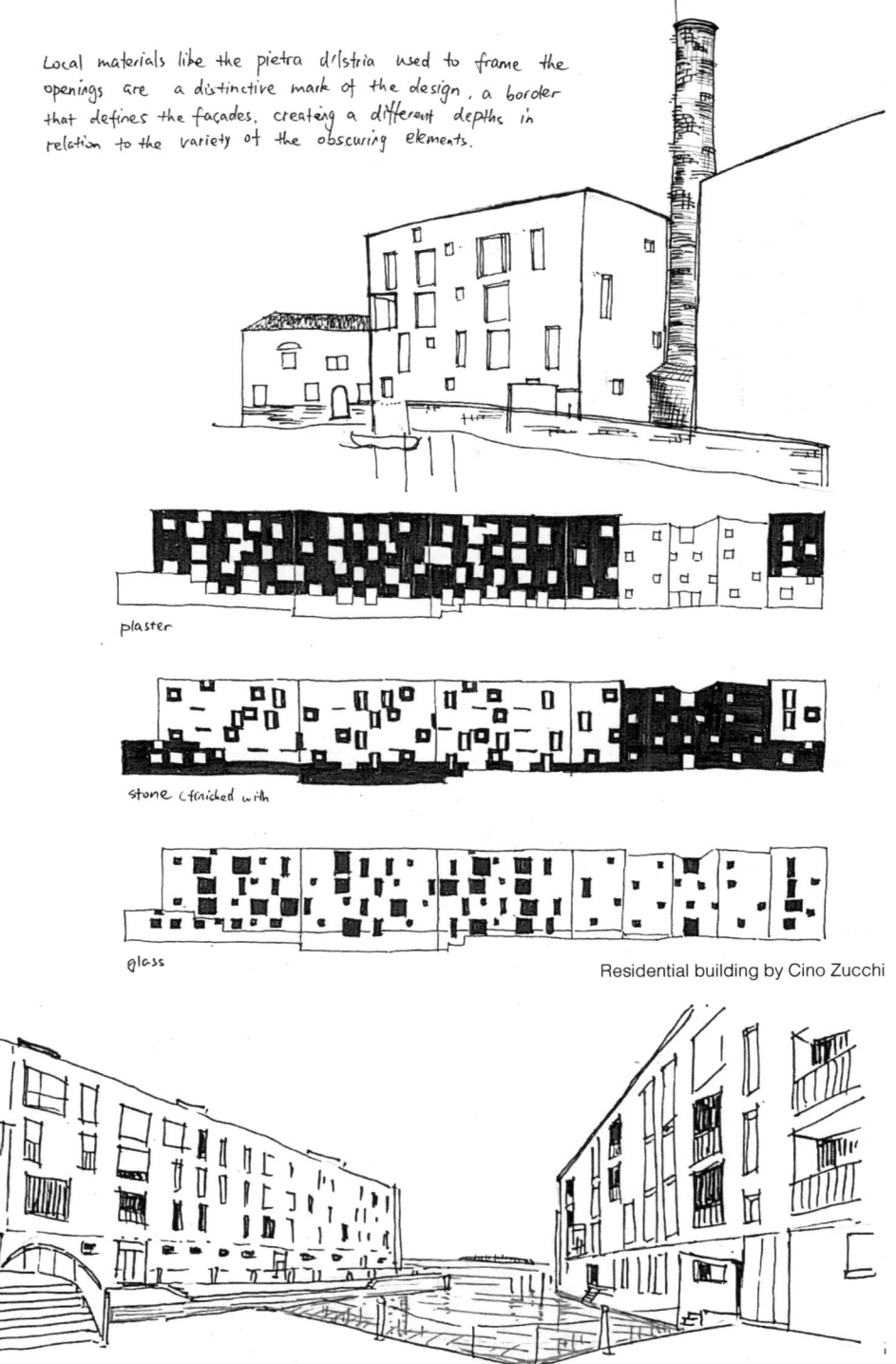

Cannaregio

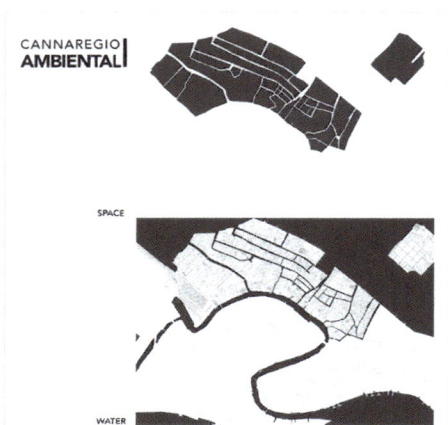

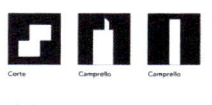

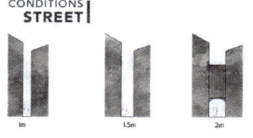

MODERN PRECEDENT
GREGOTTI

Ex Saffa Housing Complex

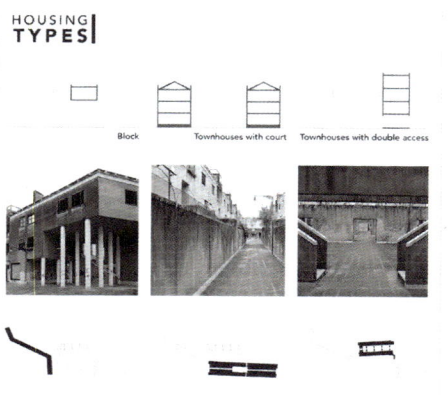

SKETCH
CAMPO SAN GEREMIA

SKETCH
GHETTO

SKETCH
RIO TERA DEI FRANSCESCHI

SKETCH
RIO DELLA SENSA

 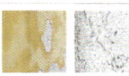

CONDITIONS **EDGE**   CONDITIONS **INTERNAL**

  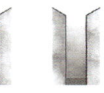 

MODERN PRECEDENT
CHIPPERFIELD
San Michele Island Cemetery

CEMETERY
SOLIDS

An organisational structure has been developed which groups volumes together to form a greater sense of settlement and enclosure

CEMETERY
VOIDS

Interplay of positive and negative space creating moments of pause and reflection

San Marco

Basilica di San Marco

Campo San Samuele

Basilica San Marco

Venice inspiring the world

Valentina Tridello Università IUAV di Venezia

In 1902, St. Mark's Bell tower in Piazza San Marco collapsed and that image bounced worldwide. Only two years later, the Metropolitan Life Tower, a 2:1 copy of the Venetian Bell Tower, was rising in the city of New York, some thousands of kilometers away. It was the first of a long series of reinterpretations of Venice. Thus, as it is acknowledged in many books and references, for example in the recent publication *Se Venezia muore*, we can argue that Venice inspires the world (Settis, 2014).

A thousand times imitated and copied, Venice today counts 97 fake twins spread throughout the world and listed in the book *Welcome to Venice*. (Moltedo, 2007) These cities are sometimes enclosed in a shopping mall, as in the case of Macao. Others like Nova Veneza in Brasil are real newly founded cities made through the effort of the Veneto's nostalgic emigrants. Some like examples in Abu Dhabi and Kundu, are resorts that "have no less but more than the real Venice" as mentioned in the slogan of the Turkish clone, "to live Venice you don't need to go there anymore". And, of course, one cannot dismiss the amusement parks and the casinos typified by the most famous case of the Las Vegas Venetian Resort Hotel.

In fact, the comparison is often made between the city and a theme park: such a perfect place to spend a vacation but not to live - so beautiful that it cannot be a true city.

For the flow of tourism in the last decade, the association of Venice with leisure and romantic times has changed completely. From earlier times, typical tourists have been mostly interested in its history, culture and the unique legacy of historic buildings. Venice is now visited by a massive number of daily visitors amounting to a total of 34 million presences in a city that can bear only 12 million (G.Tattara, 2014). Of course, the island is overloaded with people to such an extent that for each inhabitant we can proportionally count 600 tourists.

The citizens of Venice are victims of an economy that is changing completely the nature of the city itself. Crushed by high living conditions and by the disappearance of daily shops to leave space to souvenir sellers, the Venetians are leaving their island. A pharmacy in the center of the city is now taking a sarcastic account of the "diaspora" of Venetians. Taking this dramatic situation seriously, UNESCO gave an ultimatum to the municipal administration: to take good measures to confront the uncontrolled flow of tourists to avoid having Venice listed as a city at risk. Having only 55.583 inhabitants in its historic centre (La Nuova, 2016), Venice can neither compare nor compete with the 263.859 inhabitants of the mainland. In fact, the municipality of Venice also includes part of the mainland, in particular the city of Mestre. This situation has had a negative impact on the political elections concerning the vote for the mayor and the city council. In spite of the fact that the island needs the economic support from *terra firma*, it is clearly evident that with its minority the historical centre has limited political power. It is hoped that the current administration will fulfill UNESCO's request and will focus its policies on the problems of the historical city.

Indeed, the existing image of Venice as an amusement park is also the result of political choices made in the past. In 1981 Marco Romano, a professor of urbanism at the IUAV University of Venice and later, member of the superior council for Beni Culturali, wrote in the magazine Urbanistica: "The transformation of Venice in a Disneyland could mark the switchover to a more creative, happier and more joyous way of life". Of course, if this was the position taken by the main stakeholders of the last two decades, it is easy to imagine how the current situation eventually came about.

With gigantic advertisements covering its buildings, Venice is every day more similar to its clones. This provocation is also the topic of Chain City, a video exhibited during the XI Biennale of Architecture, in which the authors compared the real Venice with her copies, by showing on two different screens a gondola's trip in the real Venice and the same trip in a fake one. What are the differences? Which is the real one? By splitting herself in so many copies has Venice lost her identity? It is the fear of Marco Polo in Italo Calvino's The Invisible Cities. He is afraid he will lose the memory of Venice if he talks about it:

Photomontage of the San Marco
bell tower collapsing by Zago

Metropolitan Life Tower
1905/1907 Napoleon Le Brun

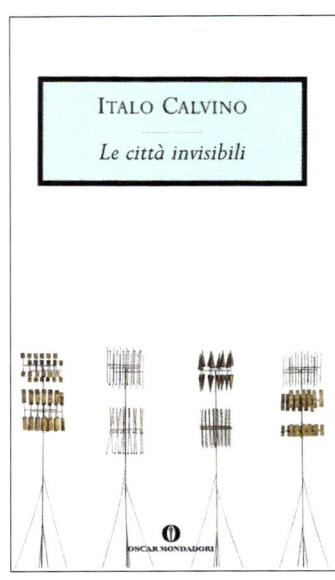

Calvino, Italo,
Le città invisibili, 1972.

"Sire, now I told you about all the cities I know."
Marco Polo bowed his head.
"Venice," the Khan said.
Marco smiled. "What else do you believe I have been talking to you about?"
The emperor did not turn a hair. "And yet I have never heard you mention that name."
And Polo said: "Every time I describe a city I am saying something about Venice."
"When I ask you about other cities, I want to hear about them. And about Venice, when I ask you about Venice."
"To distinguish the other cities' qualities, I must speak of a city that remains implicit. For me it is Venice."
"You should than begin each tale of your travels from the departure, describing Venice as it is, all of it, not omitting anything you remember of it." […]
"Memory's images, once they are fixed in words, are erased," Polo said. "Perhaps I am afraid of losing Venice all at once, if I speak of it. Or perhaps, speaking of other cities, I have already lost it, little by little."

So, Venice is not one. It has essentially multiplied. Its clones would be the copy of one of its thousand aspects, of which it will ever remain only a copy because it would never be able to steal the complexity of the soul of Venice. We could say that Venice is all the other cities, but the other cities are not Venice. That is why we often hear the name, "Venice of the north" when talking about cities such as Amsterdam or Saint Petersburg. However, we would never call Venice the "Amsterdam of the south".

And when we compare Venice with a theme park, we should recognize what all the amusement parks of the world have learned lessons from Venice. Disneyland is a world in the world, a "heterotopia" and Venice, in its way, is a heterotopia too. Still having connections with the rest of the world, the time in Venice beats to the rhythm of the pedestrian, it flows slower than in the rest of the car-based cities. If Las Vegas is the city of signs, where the architecture is a poster of itself and where the driver when catching a glimpse of himself in the mirror relates to the city through the speed of his car, then Venice is exactly the opposite.

By walking around the Venice's *calli* and *campi*, the students of the Seidler International Studio were able to appreciate the multiplicity of these details: the human interactions and the feeling of safety felt in a city with no vehicular traffic. By walking, you pay more attention to the city that is all around you, and then you care about it.

Venetians are known to be conservative people for whom it is hard to accept changes, particularly in their city. But we could read this stubbornness as an auto-preservation of the beauty of Venice. Venetians are accustomed to live and to see in their daily routine a beautiful place that would provoke the *Stendhal's syndrome*. So, how can we blame them if they are afraid of changes?

Within this scenario, it is always interesting to bring together a number of diverse architects, researchers and students who, coming from contrasting perspectives and realities, would confront and think about the unique experience that is Venice. In the following chapters, the students have analyzed remarkable buildings of the last century, to understand how architects of the modernity have challenged Venice's architectural language. Following Harry Seidler's observation of ancient architecture, which for him is capable of "developing an appropriate architecture, expressive of the artistic and technological impacts in building today," the students designed their own proposals for the borders of Venice.

Calvino, Italo, *Le città invisibili*, 1972.
Diller, Elizabeth, Ricardo Scofidio and Charles Renfro, *Chain City*, XI Mostra Internazionale di Architettura, *Out There. Architecture Beyond Building*
Mancuso, Franco, *Venezia è una città*, 2016.
Montanari, Tommaso, *Le pietre e il popolo*, 2013.
Moltedo, Guido, *Welcome to Venice*, 2007.
Scarpa, Tiziano, *Venezia è un pesce*, 2000.
Settis, Salvatore, *Se Venezia muore*, 2014.
Summers, Anna, *The Coming Death of Venice*, 2013.
Tattara, Giuseppe, *Quantify cruising. Study on the economic impact of large cruise ships in Venice*, 2014.

Diogo Pires Ferreira
youtube.com/cidadeideia credits

Venice borders
Enrico Fontanari Università IUAV di Venezia

The historic center of Venice has a Master Plan that defines strict design guidelines, generally oriented toward the conservation of the urban and building heritage. Instead, the two external areas, which could be called the two peripheral lagoon borders on the northern side along the Fondamenta Nuove toward the airport and the islands of Murano and Burano and on the southern side along La Giudecca island, have undergone several transformations from the second half of the 19th century until the end of 20th century, leaving a number of urban voids or open spaces. In the second half of the 19th century, the first industrial development of the city was concentrated at these two borders. During the 20th century they were relocated on the mainland in the area called Porto Marghera resulting in a large number of deserted areas, which merged with often abandoned, private, open spaces, particularly on the southern border of La Giudecca Island. This process of recent urban transformation has guided the Venice Master Plan to identify several areas of transformation and redevelopment, by allowing the insertion of new constructions and open spaces. These became the two design study areas for the 2015 and 2016 Seidler International Design Studio. The work realized by the students represents a good example of the implementation of design principles and methodologies proposed by Harry Seidler in his texts and lessons.

The study areas

The study areas were located on the southern border of Venice in 2015, on the Island of La Giudecca and in 2016 on the northern border of the historic city along the Fondamenta Nuove, in the neighborhoods of Castello and Cannaregio. The urban morphology and consistency in these two areas are different, but in both areas the students had the opportunity to confront interesting urban challenges and to develop different urban design proposals inserted in a complex urban context.

In particular, they had to face the relationship between their proposals and the landscape of the Lagoon of Venice. The lagoon has an extremely complex and variable nature and represents a very dense system of relations to be observed, analysed, researched and finally grasped as a *total environment*. Its boundaries and limits with the mainland and with the borders of the historic city continuously change in shape, colour, moisture and materials, according to the influence of the wind and the water level. The ground, usually submerged by the water during high or normal tide, is characterized by different vegetation and environmental typologies.

The artificial transformation of the natural environment of the lagoon into a human settlement began with the construction of a border around the islands, raising the land, cultivating it, regularizing the waterways and reclaiming more land from the water. Through these activities the Venetians started to build their landscape and their city. The city of Venice was laid out on these landscape rules. The city was built on parallel allotments and connecting water-links from one canal to another, in this way defining the structural shape of its urban morphology. The buildings and their main entrances bordered the main waterways, while the private spaces, such as service buildings, courtyards and gardens were located at the back. All were fenced in, inaccessible and hardly ever visible from the streets (*calli*) and the squares (*campi*) because they were completely surrounded by high walls. The walls of Venetian gardens are similar to a partition that closes, but at the same time opens up to important visual connections. The walls do not appear to be clear boundaries, since often windows and doors are cut into them. This is an important element that contributes to the definition of the complex relation between the public and private spaces of the city.

While designing their urban and architectural transformations of Venice's borders, students had to work with careful attention to the morphological characteristics of the *insulae*. Their design process was inclusive of delicate and perceptive sensibilities related to the landscape of the lagoon and its canals - the environmental aspects defined by the movement of the water, the changing of the light and of the vegetation, the different construction materials of the open spaces, the borders of the city and the private spaces.

The South Front: "La Giudecca"

The southern Border, located on the island of La Giudecca, is characterized by a more fragmented and soft urban sectors with a clear urban morphology based on a perpendicular north-south pedestrian circulation system. On the northern part of La Giudecca island, a *fondamenta* (large pedestrian street) facing the Giudecca Canal and the historic city, connects the entire island from east to west. From this *fondamenta* a series of *calli* (pedestrian paths) cut the island from the northern edge to the southern end toward the border of the lagoon. The building typology follows the *forma*

Aerial photo of the Island of la Giudecca

urbis defined by this system of streets and characterized by a lined up series of rectangular allotments. Therefore, the urban borders consist of a sequence of row houses, sometimes interrupted by warehouses or other productive buildings or by religious settlements. The back of the built border is in this case, defined by a large open space, often used as a garden, private or semi-public, with a special open structure on the southern border of the lagoon.

The entire southern border is defined by a number of open spaces, which are the result of abandoned industrial settlements or gardens of the old system of villas or vegetable gardens of the convents. The gardens built on the border of the lagoon are different from the ones built in the historical center, mostly because of the availability of space along the lagoon border where they could expand. Long walls enclose the gardens and these barriers set off a relationship not only with the city similar to what happens in the garden of the historical center but also with the lagoon, through a long string of windows, doors and portals which open along the southern border of the island, facing the canal and the lagoon to the south. In this part of the city, the built border alternates not only with important private gardens but also with other typologies of open spaces. A number of these open spaces are what remains of the

1 Giudecca: gardens and convents on the South Front.

2 The abandoned industrial South Front of the Giudecca.

South Giudecca new housing, design of Gino Valle (1984-86).

productive areas introduced in the 19th century, now abandoned. Other areas are productive, still in use particularly as shipyards, while some are other forms of open spaces.

A significant role of the landscape is represented by the cultivated green spaces within the monastic convents. They are built geometrically in relation to the shape of the cloister, to then fade into more natural looking spaces as the area widens up to the edge of the lagoon. The cloister is the emblematic area of the green spaces in the convent, since it is a place for prayer but also of cultivation and water collection. Rows of pergolas or of cypresses extend between these architectonic spaces and the areas of cultivation, becoming the element of conjunction between the cloister, the garden and the orchard. The borders of the gardens and the orchards coincide with the water edge of the lots, marked by docks, overlooking points, doors, shipyards, fields and slipways.

This fluctuation of built areas and green open spaces and this extension of the built walls towards the lagoon, represent a continuous opening to the city life on the land and on the water, constituting the main characteristic of the southern border.

Working in this kind of urban and natural space, the students were invited to consider Harry Seidler's design principles, not only for the built environment (single buildings survey, urban analysis, morphological aspects, etc.), but also for its relation with the natural elements. By considering the defined brick enclosures of the single gardens or of the entire southern border, they had to face the contradiction created by the changes of the water level and its effects on these borders, which are never clear nor well defined. The water changes the landscape of the city, and the border seems hard. Instead, however, it is an extremely soft and variable element. All these tensions have been reflected well in the students' design proposal described in the following chapters.

J. De Barbari (1500)
Detail of Venice's North Front

The North Front: "Fondamenta Nuove"

The project area chosen by the workshop of 2016 is situated along the northern border of Venice, an area of the city with strong potential for changes. The northern area of the city has always been considered as a peripheral zone of the city's center, confirmed by the interventions undergone up until the first half of the 20th century. Today a series of changes in the interpretation of the city's islands, and above all in the current evaluation of the transport system from the mainland to the city center, are helping to reveal the potential of this area as a future meeting ground for a new urban polarity. In this area of the lagoon, between the mainland border and the northern border of the historic city, characterized by the large pedestrian walk of the Fondamenta Nuove, there are numerous areas and sites, which are suitable for the realization of new important urban interventions. Some have already been realized, like the Tessera Airport on the mainland or the renovation of the Civic Hospital on the Fondamenta Nuove, some are still interested by important actions of restoration and urban renewal, like the island of Murano and the large area of the Arsenale of Venice. In their approach to the project sites of the ex-Gasometer complex, the orchards of San Francesco della Vigna, the open spaces of La Celestia and a number of buildings belonging to the Arsenale, students had to take into account the historical and morphological evolution of these sites as well as their new urban potential. This has become more and more evident in recent years and is a key aspect in the local government's planning activities for the territory.

Originally, the northern border of Venice was a semi-marshy zone, a true outskirt, which lacked a clear demarcation from the lagoon to the north. It was a zone mainly used for storage by fishermen and by timber transporters. Over the course of the 13th century large monasteries and convents of minor orders were founded along this undefined edge, such as San Francesco della Vigna, San Giovanni

View of the North Front of Venice, with the Arsenal in foreground and the Islands of San Michele (the cemetery of the city) and Murano in background

e Paolo, Santa Maria della Misericordia, la Madonna dell'Orto and San Alvise. Traditionally, the monasteries were established in parts of the city, which were considered peripheral, in some way to give assistance to the poverty-stricken residents of these areas and also to reclaim the land and enhance its value. The establishment of these religious settlements along the northern periphery also resulted in the creation of vast cultivable areas and gardens (like in the southern border) as well as rationalizing the area and maintaining the delicate system of the canals.

This situation was radically modified in the 16th century, with the first important intervention in the area: the construction of the Fondamenta Nuove and a bordering canal, whose main function was to protect the northern part of the city from lagoon erosion. In this way, a hard, stone and brick, rigid border, definitively transformed the originally soft border of the city. However, this intervention, that responds to a more general city objective and belongs to a series of urban transformative interventions issued by the Venetian Government in the 1500s, does not change but rather confirms the peripheral condition of this area: an area that used to be located between the undefined northern border of the Cannaregio neighborhood and the large, inaccessible complex of the Arsenale.

Over the course of the 19th century other interventions were taking place in this area, following the trend of a city that was trying to "modernize" itself. The most important interventions being the creation of the large city cemetery on the island of San Michele, the new Civic Hospital, the construction of the Gasometer complex and the internal changes made to the Arsenale. Some of these interventions included the demolition of a bridge, which linked the Gasometer with the Fondamenta Nuove, contributed to the isolation of the north-western portion of Venice, closed off on one side by the Arsenale and with few means of connection with the rest of the city on the other side. Finally, the marginality of this area was further reinforced by several interventions undergone in the 1900s.

Thanks to the new Masterplan of the City of Venice, approved at the end of the 20th century, this part of the city was finally seen from a new perspective. Other significant transformations that changed the role of Venice's northern border include the renewal and enlargement of the Tessera Airport and the proposal to reorganize the points of access to the city center by the creation of two new terminals on the mainland: one to the south (Fusina) and one to the north (Tessera). The idea of the northern zone becoming the city's main access point for people arriving from the airport and from the mainland modifies and increases the potential of the zone: a number of areas would be available to be converted into current or future cultural activities. The presence of highly strategic zones and activities and the prevision of a new access route to the city's center would begin an urban transformation that would help to re-balance the current city center and the heavy dependence on the western side of the city (railway station, bus terminal of Piazzale Roma, offices, etc.).

This was the framework the students had to keep in mind while approaching the design proposal for this area. At the same time, they had to recognize the significant impact on this area of its residential use characterized by a significant social housing neighbourhood - probably one of the largest in the city. The diverse uses would contribute to the creation of a particular social mixité, unique in the historic city, by characterizing this area as an important residential zone of the historic city. In the consideration of the past history, the current social and natural context and the future potential transformation, the students had to keep in mind two important aspects: the zone is becoming one of the "doors" to the city, typified by several urban landmarks from the Misericordia

1 Satellite photo of Venice and the Lagoon North

2 Accessibility proposed by the new Masterplan of 1994-98

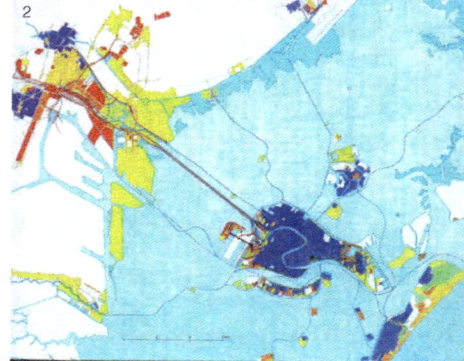

Church to the abandoned area of the Gasometer, and there are important urban roles performed by the civic hospital and the Arsenal. At the same time this is a border area, a sort of window onto the lagoon. When studying and designing for such an area, the traditional methods of treating the lagoon structures (such as the brick walls, the stone edges, the foundations, etc.) would have been considered. However, it was also important to pay attention to the aesthetic potential of the area, because this is a zone in which one can admire the seascape of the lagoon, with its antique structures (the islands) and the new projects (enlargement of the San Michele cemetery).

These considerations, taken together with the acknowledgement of the restrictions and conditions involved, made the design issues of 2016 fertile and of particular interest, obliging the students to base their design proposal on a serious critical study of the complex equilibrium between the area's functional needs, the important residential role and its aesthetic qualities. Their formal design solutions tried to address the view of the morphological aspects of the northern border of Venice that Giancarlo De Carlo expressed in an effective sentence: "It is a "line" that takes up different configurations as it unfolds from west to east….." [1].

---

[1] G. De Carlo, *Fondamenta Nuovissime*, in Fondamenta Nuovissime, ILA&UD, Venezia, 2000.

The South Front

The Workshop took place at Palazzo Badoer in Venice from November 23th to December 4th, 2015.

PROFESSORS: Enrico Fontanari (IUAV), Paola Favaro (UNSW), James Weirick (UNSW), Lisa Zamberlan (UNSW). Tutor: Anna-Paola Pola (IUAV)

STUDENTS: Caterina Barbon, Temyka Belgrove, Alicia Bell, Simone Bet, Taya Brooks, Nick Bucci, Tea Capoia, Francesco Ceola, Piera Favaretto, Davide Grandi, Alice Gruarin, Anthony Ho, Siyi Huang, Aghjeh Kandi, Ruoyu Li, Haihong Liu, Wei Liu, Michelangelo Mezzocolli, Michela Napolitano, Samereh Nouri, Jacqueline Oliver, Silvia Pellizzon, Francesca Perer, Leonardo Peressa, Janice Quach, Devon Rees, Thida Sachathep, Chiara Semenzin, Chelsea Sheriden, Yujia Tao Wei Peng, Elise Vanden Dool, Matteo Vianello, Leslie Xueshen Shen, Janice Yeung Yan Xie, Yushan Yue, Paige Zhang, Yizhan Zhang.

"La Giudecca"

City in the City

GIUDECCA IS LOCATED at the south of the central islands of Venice, just across the Giudecca Canal.

Since it has been always seen as a periphery of the historic, untouchable center, Giudecca collected all the experimentation that could not been achieved in Venice.

It is important to underline that Palladio's projects are San Giorgio and Redentore churches allowed by the Venice government to be built outside Venice on the Giudecca shore.

During the 19th century, this island became the location for large homes and as a result of lack of land in the main island, the location for the first industrial buildings like Mulino Stucky and Fortuny factory.

At present time, more abandoned spaces can be found at Giudecca.

Bird's eye view of the whole area with the students projects included.

Masterplan of the whole area designed by the students. Numbered from 1 to 5 the study areas assigned to each group.

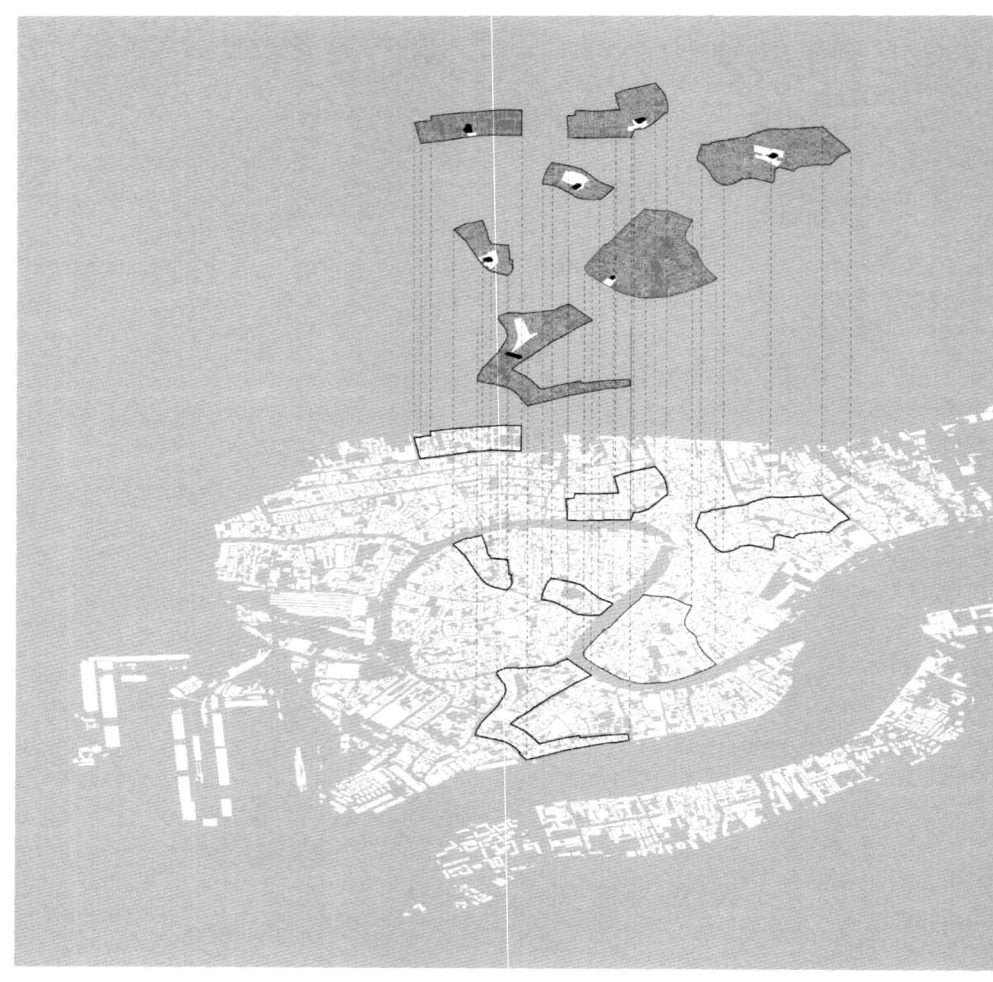

Strengths. The location of Giudecca can be one of significant opportunities in our project. The six project areas on the south border of Giudecca Island face the lagoon and the beautiful foreshore views. Abandoned and underused industrial areas have been already transformed into a number of private and public activities to include residential, hotel and artist studios.

Weakness. Some connections were missing between each separated area.

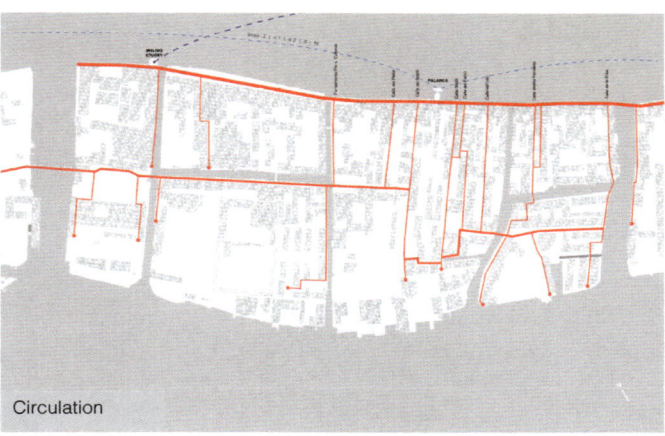

Circulation

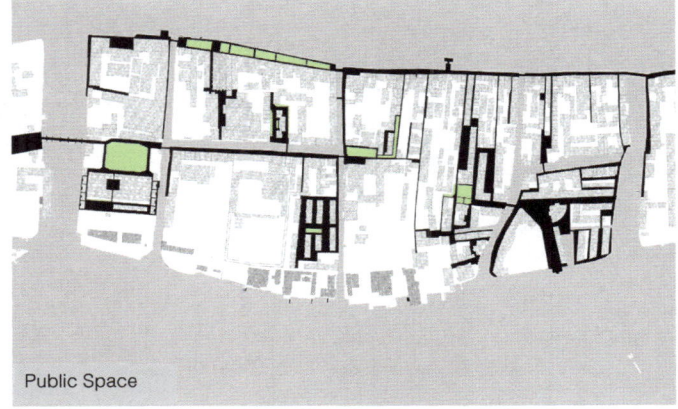

Public Space

Diagrams of the whole area: Circulation, Public Space and Functions:

- 🟡 art gallery
- 🟠 commercial spaces
- 🔴 prison
- 🟣 religious buildings
- 🟪 artisans work spaces
- 🔵 hotels
- 🟦 restaurants
- 🟢 school
- ⚫ residential buildings

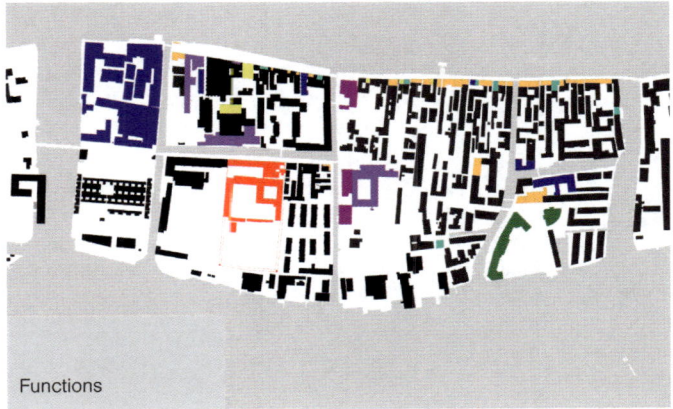

Functions

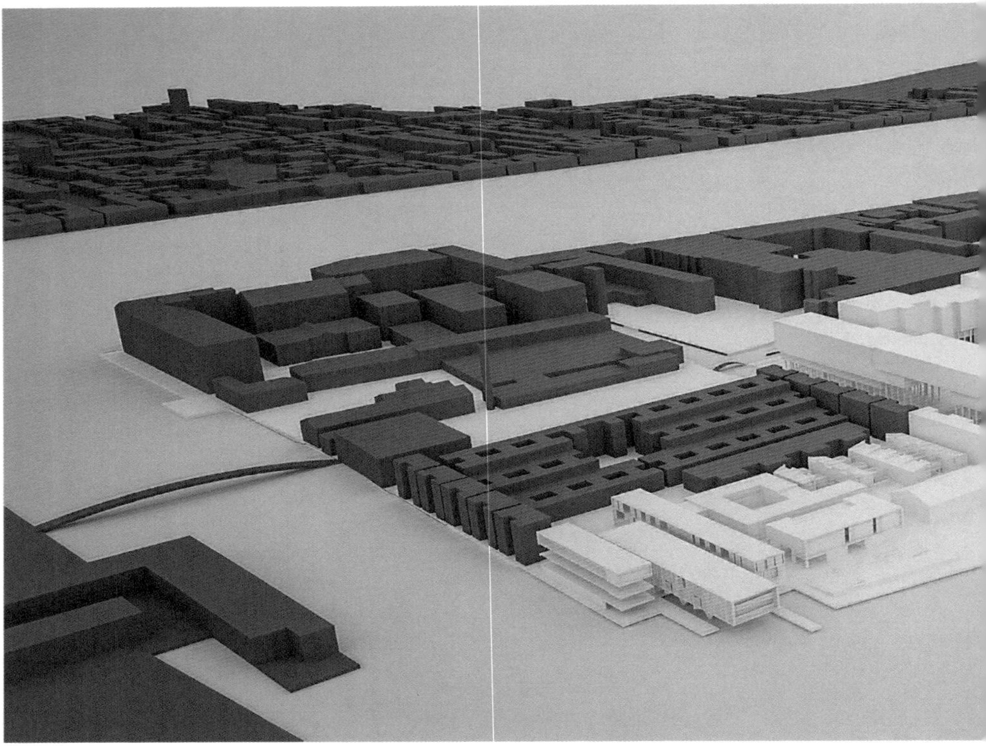

Bird's eye view of the whole
area with the students
projects included.

Caterina Barbon
Davide Grandi
Francesco Ceola
Haihong Liu
Matteo Vianello
Yujia Tao

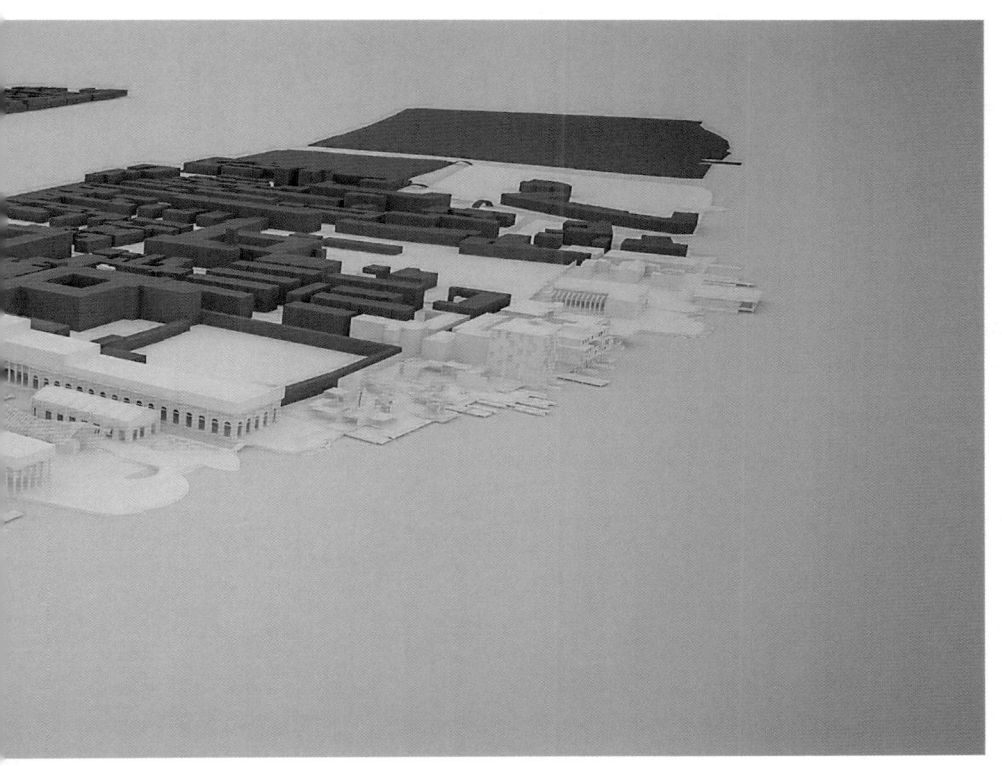

Design description and Strategy

The historic development of Venice is related to the development of formerly independent little urban settlement, still recognizable on the urban tissue through a precise relationship of spaces inside the city. The transition and the connections between public and private create here a unique mix of new spaces, which create the typical typology of Venice. The campo, an open space that collects all the primary function of every former settlement of the city, is the center of the social and commercial life.

In our design proposal of master plan group, we are trying to continue the idea of 'City in the city' in Giudecca.

We are not only to re-use the abandoned industrial lands, but also to improve the whole services in Giudecca with the better connection, transportation and way-finding system. In addition, we focused on the different functions and densities in each project areas, and tried to find the best solution by the combination of the designs.

Open Theatre
sanpolo

Tea Capoia
Ruoyu Li
Wei Liu
Wei Peng
Leonardo Peressa
Chiara Semenzin
Yizhan Zhang

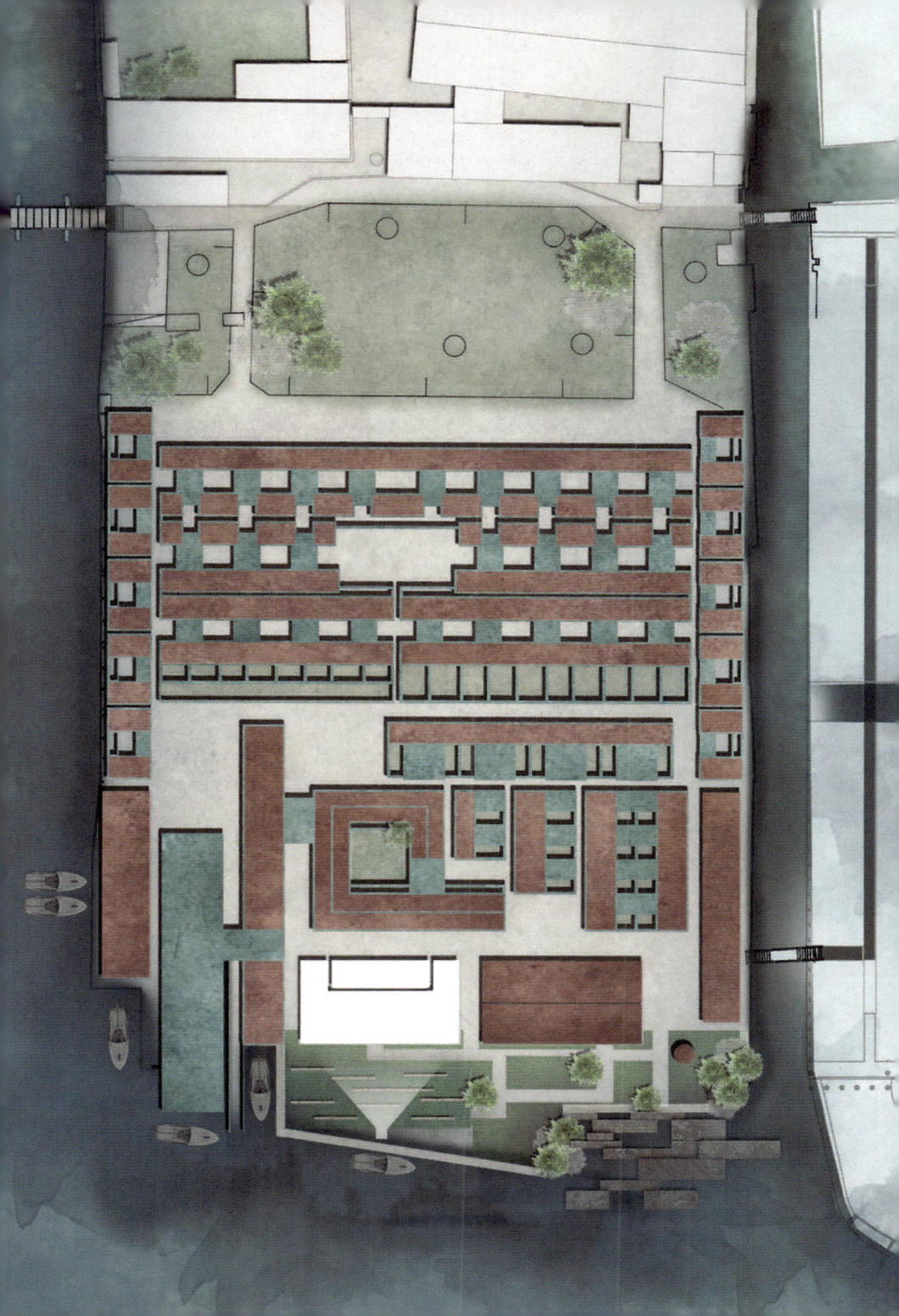

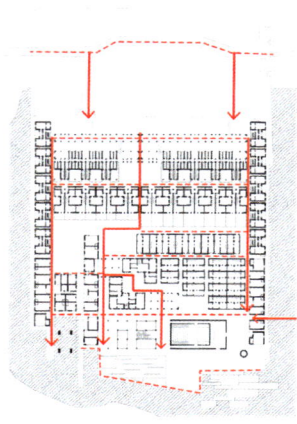

Proposed grounfloor
Main Circulation

We had a special experience during this 2 weeks collaborating studies. The first week in Venice, as design students with architectural eyes, we tried to explore the definition of venetian style.

This first two tasks we did are the historical and contemporary analysis of Venice architecture. It is a different ideology compares to what we learnt from Sydney. The narrow street, the arch corridor, and the large scaled campo spaces.

Moving to our design, once we heard from our venetian students about the open theatre they had in the past. The conceptual idea of bringing back their memories of the open theatre came out of our mind. Combining with the historical studies of Campo della Pescheria, we decided to locate the open space near the waterfront.

In order to link the open spaces with the existing **Gino Valle**'s Project, we tried to create a transmission space in between. Then we started to analysis the Gino Valle's project, which is quite useful for us to determine the orientation and the building form.

The next challenge is to involve the existing heritage building into our design proposal and give it a new function. As the harsh discussion we had, we decided to mirror a new contemporary building right next to it with a similar footprint. We provide the new function of classical theatre to the existing heritage building and tried to preserve its façade.

On the purpose of creating a contrast between these two buildings, we designed solid and void spaces into the new theatre building. Not only the differences between the building volumes, but also the materials. The strong comparison between the old brick façade with the cotton steel and channel glass.

The last and the most difficult and complex part was to create the link with the open space, the water and the building blocks. The main purpose of designing this open area was to offer the activity in relation to water and the open theatre. Therefore, we provided a sitting terrace integrated with the green areas and the open theatre screen projected on the façade of the contemporary theatre building.

We designed the terrace stairs into the water with the different rhythm of height in order to build the relation to the water. In this way, we do not only soften the edge of our site, but also create a connection to the neighbour site.

Throughout the project, the three highlights of this project is designing an open theatre space in a residential area by referring back to the existing heritage and residential buildings, forming the landscape in order to link land, water and people, at the same time involving Harry Seilder's thinking of elevating building levels in order to provide open spaces.

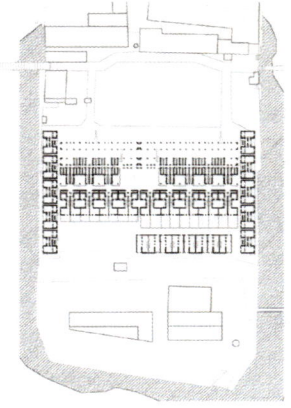
Existing groundfloor
Gino Valle's project

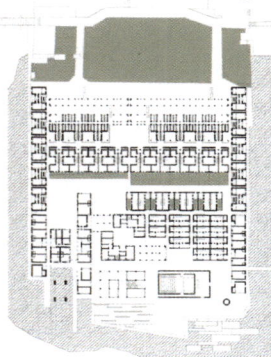
Proposed groundfloor
Public Garden

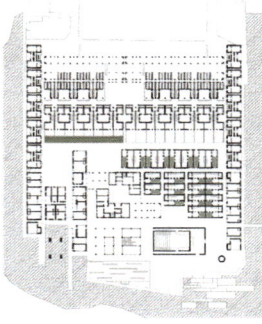
Proposed groundfloor
Secret Garden

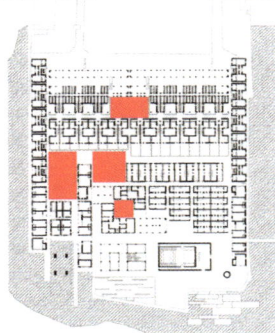
Proposed groundfloor
Campo

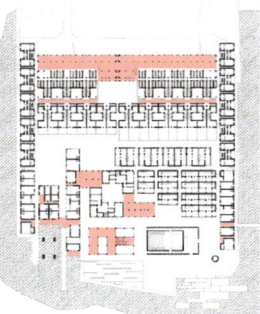
Proposed groundfloor
Sottoportego

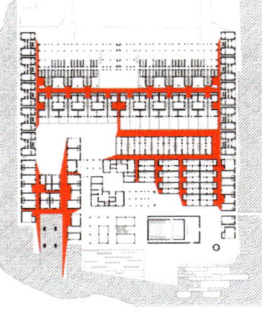
Proposed groundfloor
Street Connection

Diagram site proposal
- 8 stories
- 7 stories
- 6 stories
- 5 stories
- 4 stories
- 3 stories
- 2 stories
- 1 stories
- green
- circulation

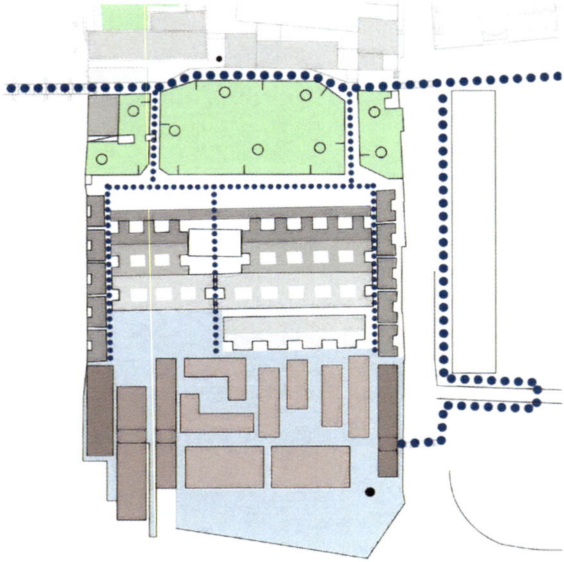

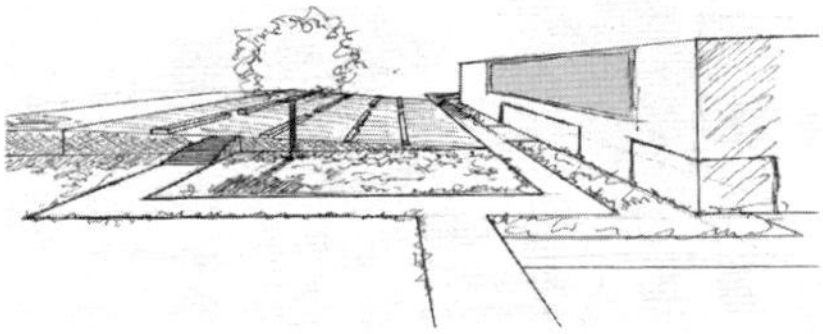

LEFT: Diagram of the general masterplan. Cross section of the island of Giudecca, form the Molino Stucky, through the Gino Valle's work, to the area of project.
View from the south lagoon.

ABOVE: Study design sketches

Urban Block
dorsoduro

Temyka Belgrove
Simone Bet
Anthony Ho
Michela Napolitano
Janice Quach
Devon Rees
Leslie Xueshen Shen

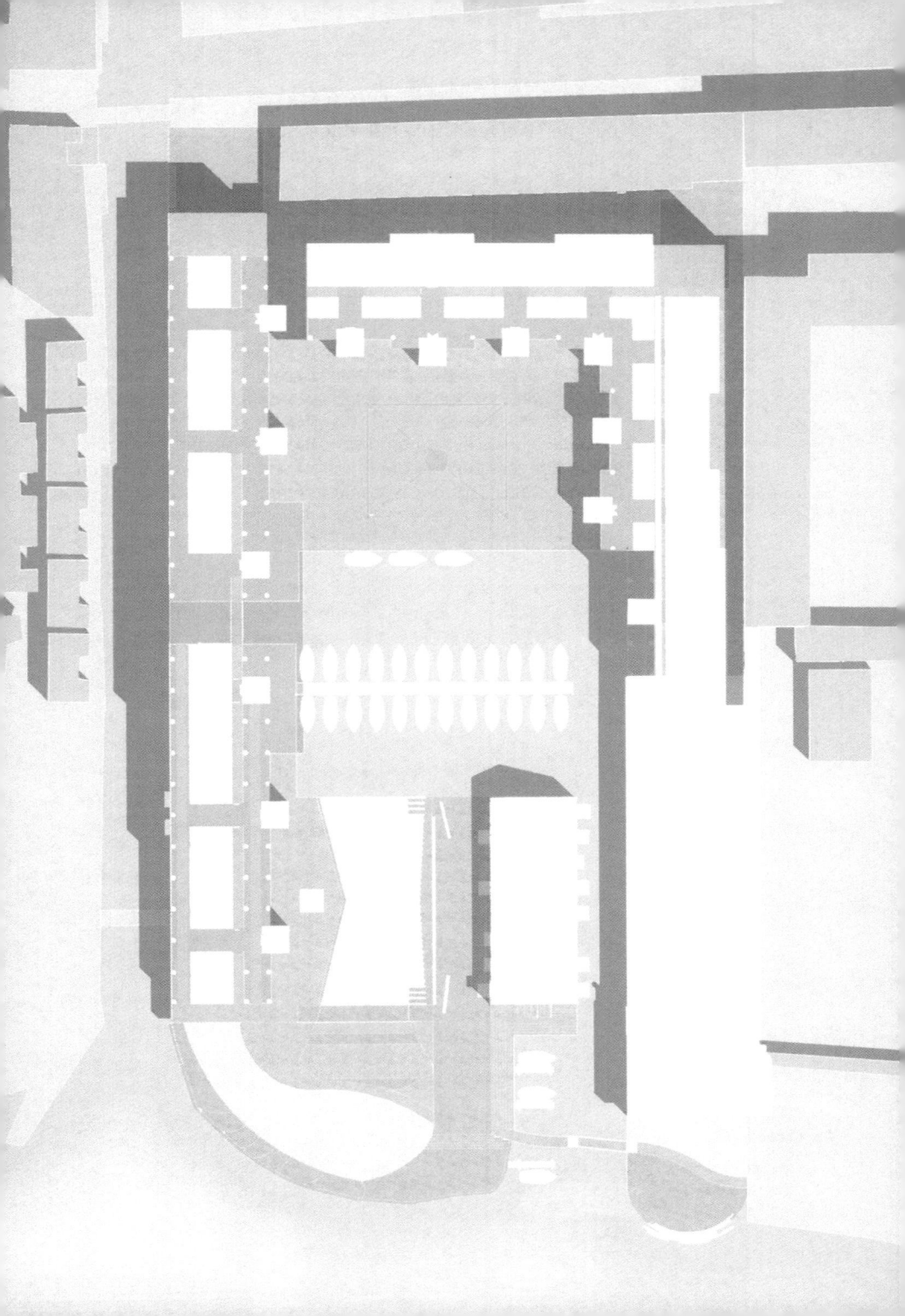

SITE TWO currently exists as an empty space with a small residential building on the northern and western boundaries. Due to being an empty site and the largest of the five sites, our initial discussion was centred around what amenity our site could bring to the existing residents of Giudecca, future residents, tourists and what responsibility we had to the other sites adjacent.

Whilst creating our scheme, research and strong influence was taken from the Biennale, Arsenale, observation of the Dorsoduro sestiere and how venetians and tourists interact with the spaces, the canals and the history of how the city of Venice was constructed upon oak piles.

In essence, our **design proposal** is broken down into five core precincts being residential, retail, landscape, public and the arts precinct. At the heart of these precincts, and the core element of our design is an internal harbour. A strong design decision was made to connect the harbour to the lagoon through creating an additional canal. This canal then became a critical factor in the servicing of the arts precinct, retail precincts and the method of arrival for most people. The harbour was developed further to include parking, boat sharing and cavane.

The retail element forms three of the borders around the campo and harbour with the residential component situated above almost appearing to be floating on pilotis, connecting to the ground through

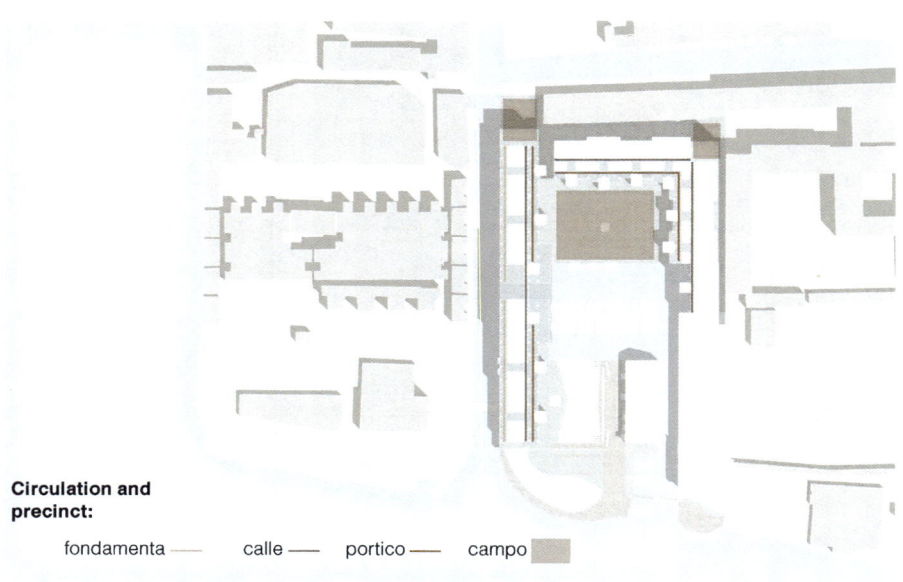

Circulation and precinct:

fondamenta ——   calle ——   portico ——   campo

Study sketches and diagrams of circulation and progam.

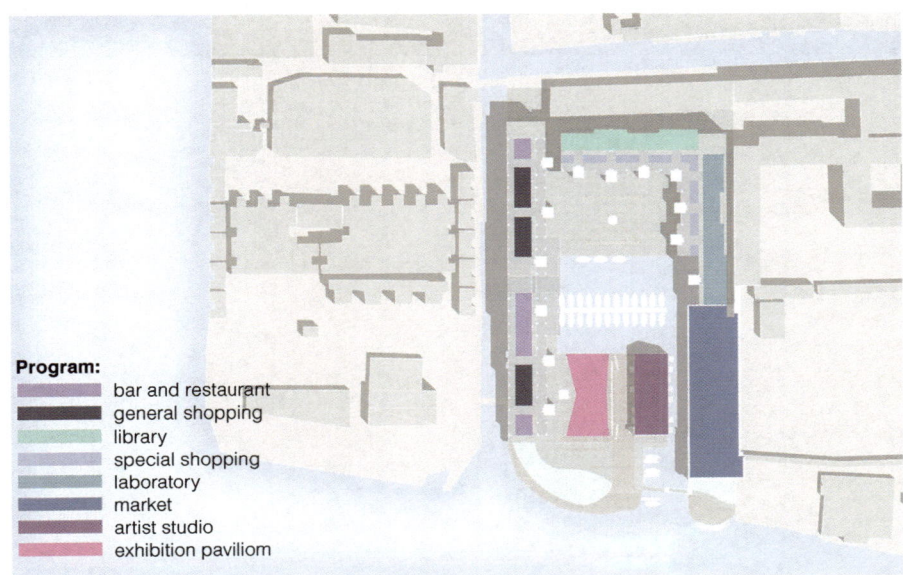

Program:
- bar and restaurant
- general shopping
- library
- special shopping
- laboratory
- market
- artist studio
- exhibition paviliom

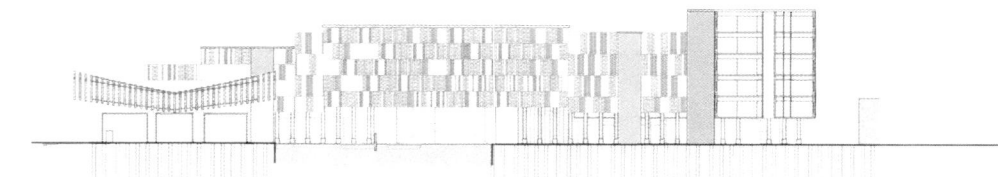

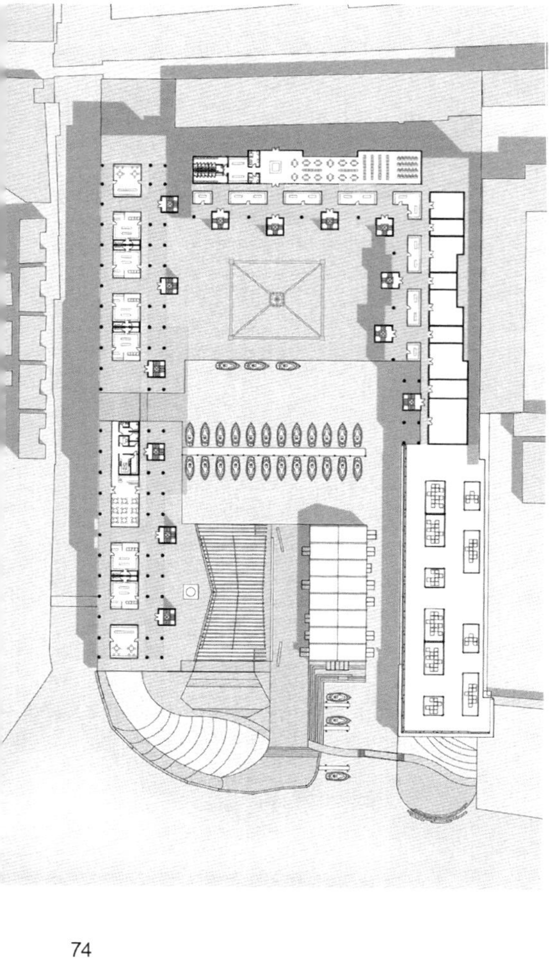

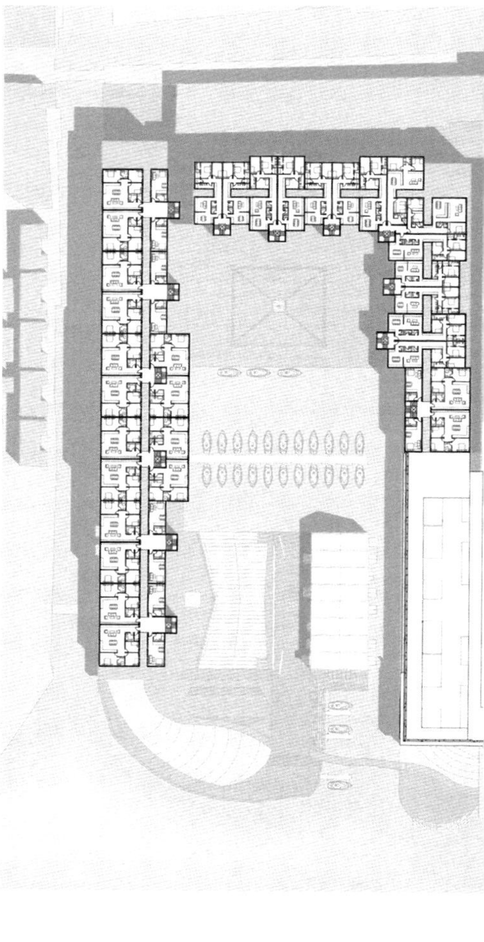

Cross section, masterplan ground floor and typical residential floor

oak piles that have risen from the lagoon. These also form a regular colonnade that references traditional Venetian built fabric.

The retail precinct includes boutique speciality stores, artisan and craftmanship stores, clothing shops, eateries and restaurants and a market to service Giudecca.

The residential precinct of the design incorporates five types of dwellings that come together through the use of calle and light wells. The calle is informed by the retail below in order to form a direct relationship. The residential buildings are a modern interpretation of Venetian housing with a layering of private and public spaces. The residential component incorporates a double skin facade with operable environmentally conscious timber composite screens.

The artist precinct is the most unique precinct in the site as it allows for a greater exploration into architecture and how we could relate Seidler's principles of geometry and art and architecture working as one element, as well as influences from the Biennale and Arsenale. The precinct consists of two primary buildings

and a thoroughfare that responds directly to the landscape and the harbour. The primary building which is the exhibition building is an irregular shape that expands and contracts as you walk through the site. The use of solid and void is pivotal in the space shown through the use of double height spaces and enclosed intimate spaces. The adjacent building is a more regular building inspired by traditional Venetian warehouses. The interior redefines how a 'warehouse' could be used and plays with the ideas of solid and void, and regularity in the design, particularly through the use of materials.

The landscape component incorporates a green landscape belt along the edge of the site with a fondamenta allowing for connection to the adjacent sites as well as creating a soft edge.

The landscaping of the precinct has a direct relationship to the arts precinct through giving the artists ownership over the sculpture garden. Boats can also arrive and park directly onto this space in addition to the harbour. The primary idea within this precinct was to create a subtle layering and thoroughfare. Overall our proposal is driven by people, and how people will interact with and use the space.

Proposal perspective of exterior spaces and view from the lagoon

Counter point
cannaregio

Alicia Bell
Nick Bucci
Elise Vanden DoolA
Thida Sachathep
Francesca Perer
Silvia Pellizzon

OUR DESIGN PROCESS was underpinned by a series of urban investigations and precedent studies, looking at both the architectural typology that exists in Venice's historical heart, and more specific contemporary projects that have been integrated into this existing fabric.

An analysis of the Cannaregio region informed our understanding of public spaces, 'Campos', and circulation in a Venetian context.

More contemporary projects by Chipperfield and Gregotti furthered our understanding of both successful and unsuccessful intervention into the Venetian fabric, reinforcing the recurring ideas of layering, spatial hierarchy, and "counterpoint" have been reinforced by our own exploration of Venice and architectural history.

Our proposal for the Giudecca site, **Counterpoint**, seeks to re-imagine the Venetian typology in a contemporary intervention that both connects the adjoining residential projects, but also serves as a recreational hub for the foreshore are.

Drawing inspiration from our precedents and urban understanding of Venice the project is articulated through an architectural language of 'pushing and pulling' creating a playful landscape of terraced platforms, trafficable pavilions, and public parks.

The intervention caters to a local community of diverse needs and hence presents a series of diverse opportunities. Visitors are encouraged to use the space as a circulatory highway, a local marketplace, or simply public spaces to inhabit at their leisure.

The proposal was developed with reference to a refined material palette, one that explores the existing Venetian condition of 'layering' and seeks to amplify this experience in a contemporary context.

Heavy concrete blades sit firmly scattered throughout the site, contrasted by a series of light operable timber screens. The combination of both elements in counterpoint create a series of open pavilions, limited only by the 'spatial imagination' of the users.

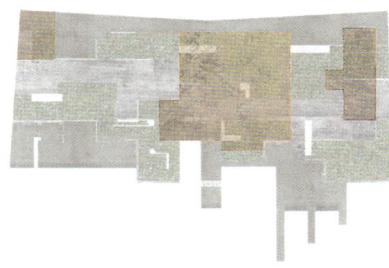

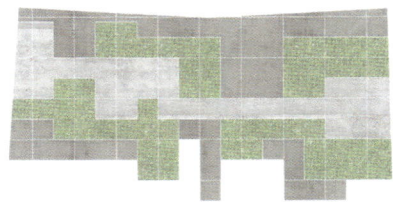

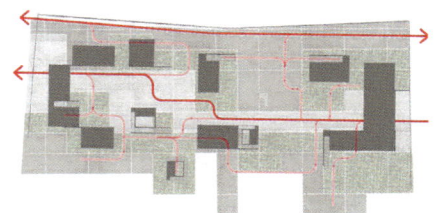

LEFT: sketches of the Giudecca island and of the study area

THIS PAGE: design view and diagrams of existing buildings (in gold), grid floor plan and circulation

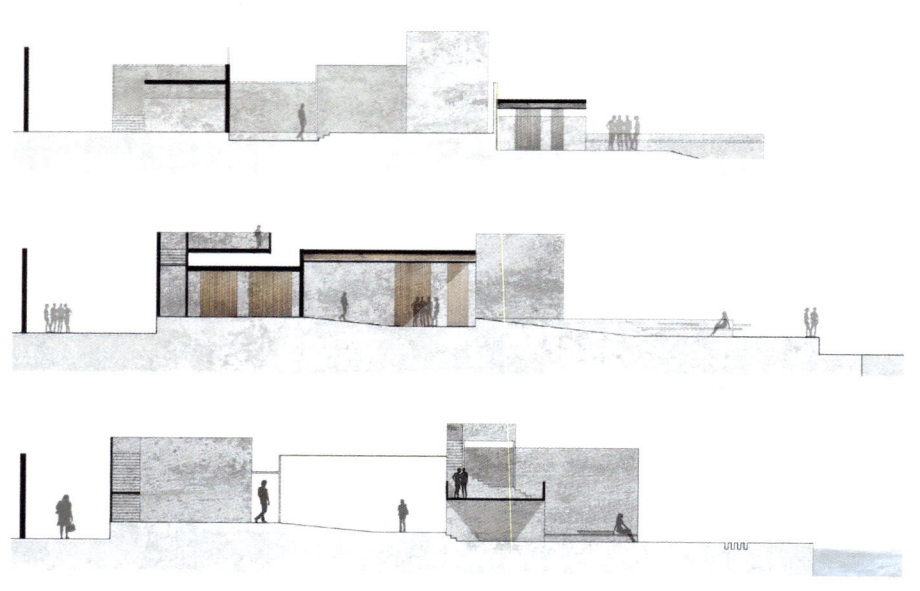

Fine detailing and a careful consideration of light and spatial interaction expresses the many lessons learnt through both our analysis and re-interpretation of Venice's constantly changing urban condition and the architectural ideology of architects such as Carlo Scarpa and Harry Seidler.

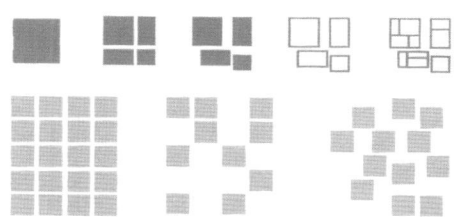

LEFT: perspective view
and sections of the project
proposed

THIS PAGE: concept modules
diagram and ground plan

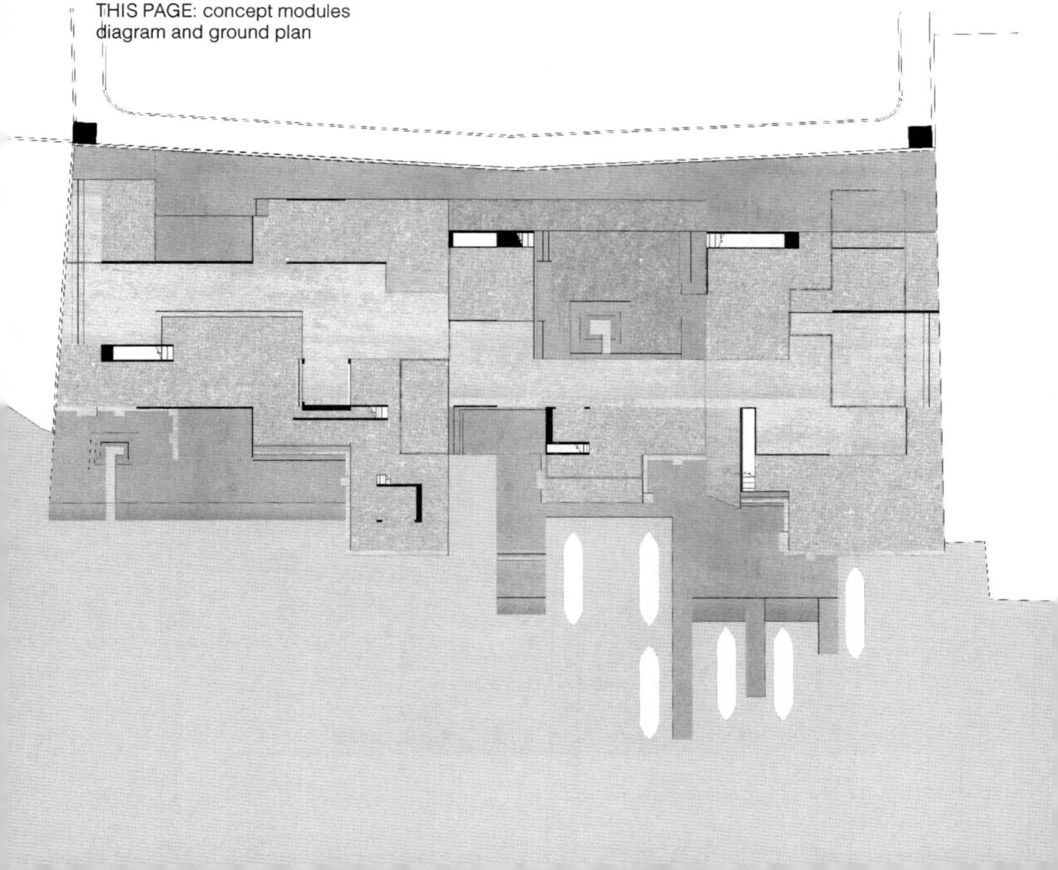

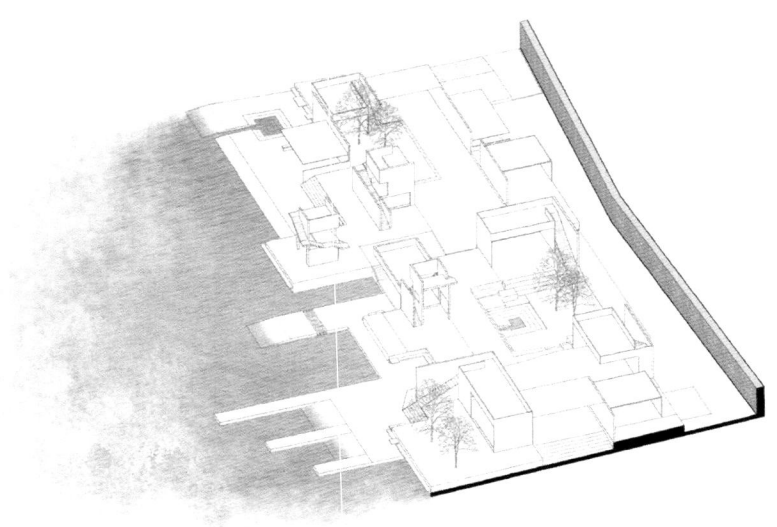

Axonometry of overall proposal, view from the south lagoon and from the fondamenta

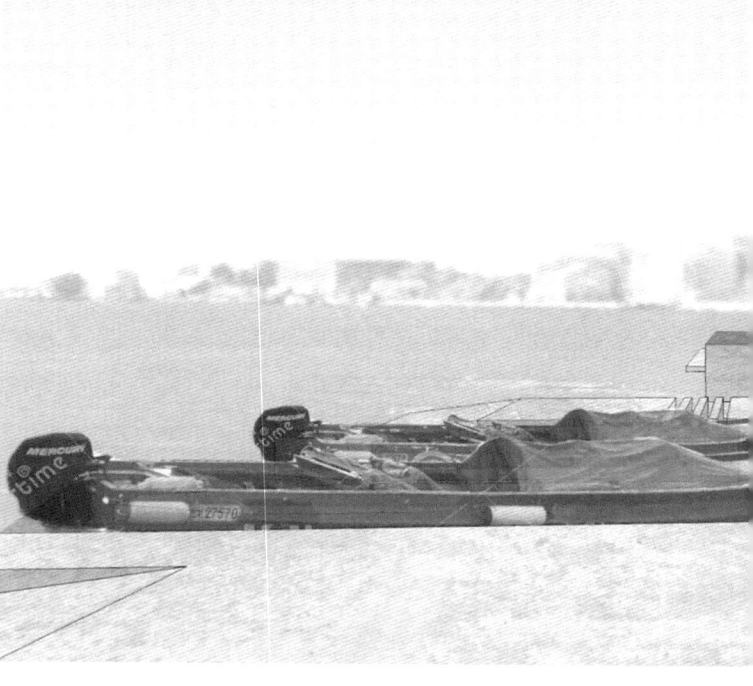

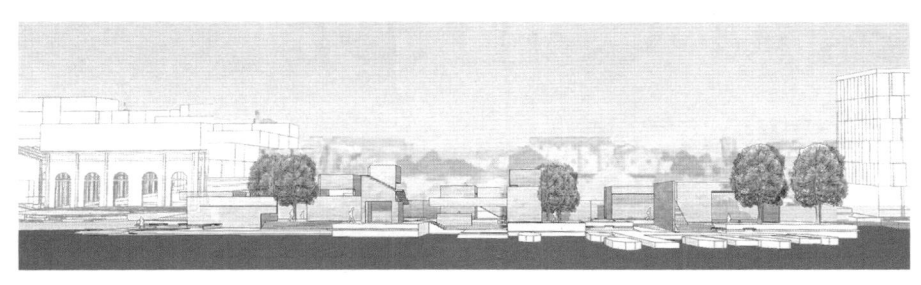

City of Corridors and Campi
sanmarco

Janice Yeung
Yan Xie
Piera Favaretto
Alice Gruarin
Yushan Yue
Siyi Huang

In this two weeks we are very grateful to have the opportunity to study Venice, a wonderful and unparalleled city. As an island, Venice is a place with limited land, hence inhibiting its ability to growth. We think the city has to become modern while acknowledging its rich historic fabric.

In Giudecca we aim to bring locals and visitors together in reinventing the area by incorporating regional techniques and materials, communicating with the context at the same time developing a new spatial dialogue.

Our analysis is based around critically assessing Venetian qualities of historical and modern buildings of our precedent study and how we discover new possibilities for our project site from this.

Our site has great potential and opportunities to landscape, architecture and interior design, as it has the advantage of

Diagrams,
Oppurtunities and
Constriants existing

THIS PAGE: design proposal overview
NEXT PAGE: cross section of the proposal, sketch and drawing

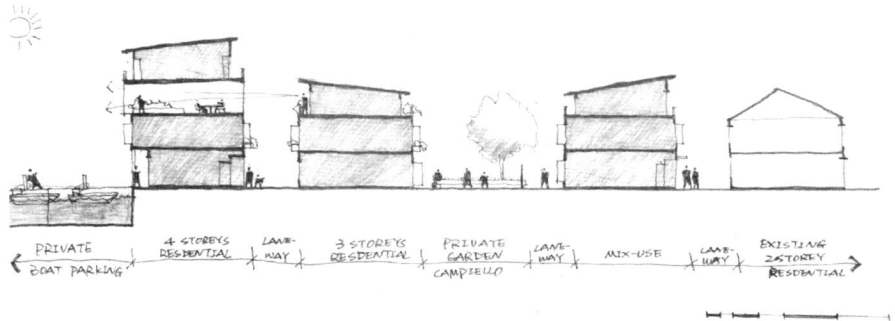

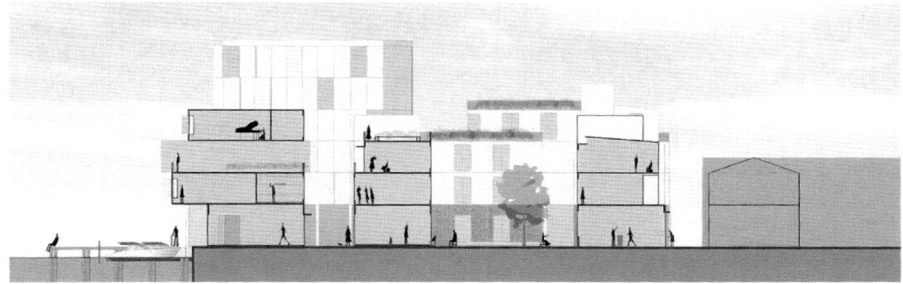

facing the Venice Lagoon towards the southern sun. It enjoys an unobstructed panoramic view with a beautiful landscape.

This opportunity has become one of the major strategies to realise the aim of our project: with an outward looking design, positive and negative spaces of built forms and open areas such as corridors try to extend themselves either physically or with the visual connection, to the water as they want to permeate it.

We believe that Venetian landscapes are all to be discovered step by step by walking through narrow corridors with high walls, and through these experience of discovering new views every step the frame of landscape changes and one eventually arrives in the bigger and open space of a campo.

Quite the contrary to the main island of Venice, which is a more commercial and tourist-oriented destination, we saw Giudecca as a more intimate and romantic residential island.

In order to retain the beauty of it, we hope to support the locals by providing a gathering space with facilities provided mainly for local Giudeccans.

With a small site and relatively high density built forms, we aim to achieve community engagement thus fostering the local spirit; and also offer Giudeccans with exclusive services such as cafè, bars, a bath house and many more.

This course has been very innovative and informative in inspiring Australian students to plan and design for an exotic context; and has also allowed Venetian students to learn from an Australian architect how to explore design solutions for their city.

Most importantly, it is through the fruitful fusion of ideas between these two parties that has enabled this project to come true.

View of the proposal
from the south lagoon

Influx
castello

Chelsea Sheriden
Paige Zhang
Jacqueline Oliver
Taya Brooks
Michelangelo Mezzocolli
Samereh Nouri Aghjeh Kandi

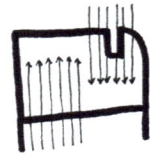
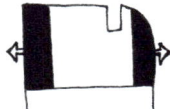
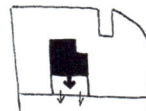
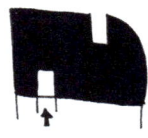
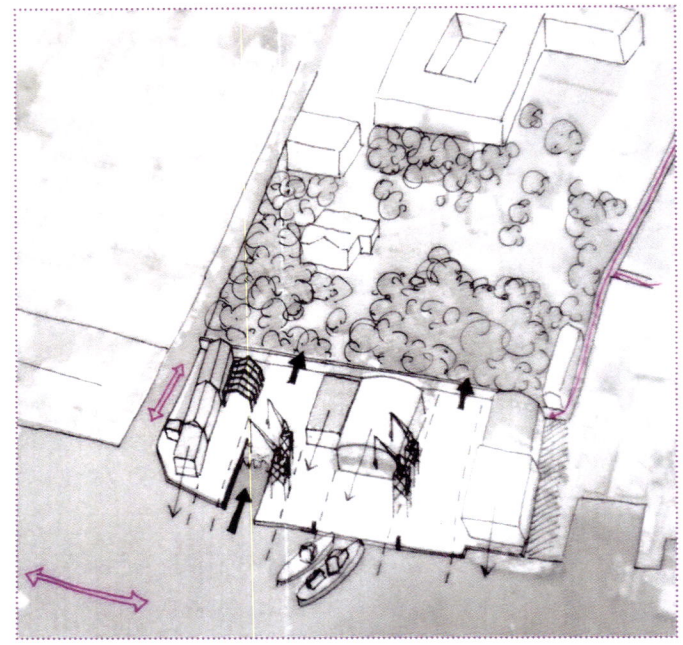

ABOVE: Concpet diagrams of the design strategies and sketch of the existing.

BELOW: study sketches of the section and the roof of the proposed buildings

INFLUX STRIVES to blur the boundaries between built and natural, tourist and local, historic and contemporary. Made up of a Canottieri club, lagoon restaurant and luxury boutique hotel.

Our scheme is not a place for transit but rather the new Guidecca destination.

The concept is based on thorough analysis of the Venetian tidal patterns over the past decade, coupled with the inverted footprint of the existing dwellings.

The Influx development is contextually and visually rich.

A detailed and well thought about landscape creates a haven for both tourist and local; revitalising the once forgotten forshore and bringing new purpose to the island of Guidecca.

Influx will allow individuals to appreciate the beauty that this island has to offer.

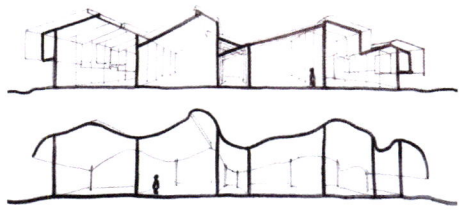

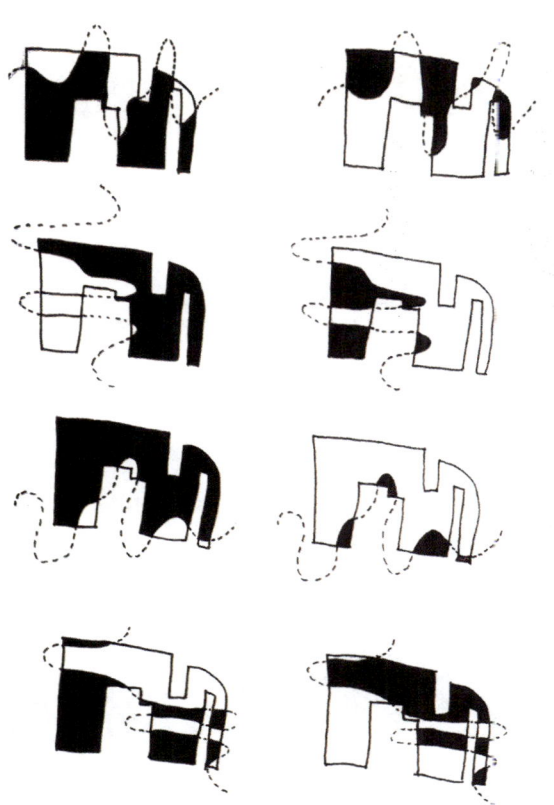

Diagrams on the design concept: movement and blur of boundaries.

BELOW: Sketch of masterplan and program

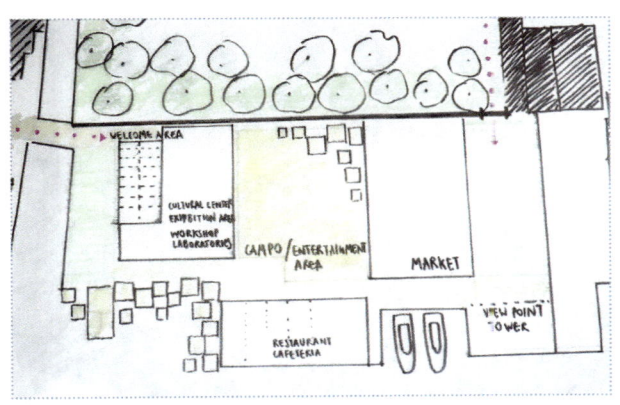

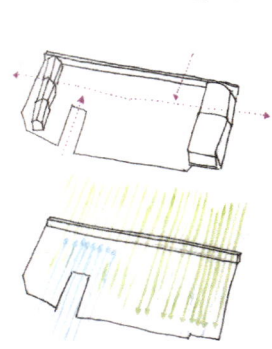

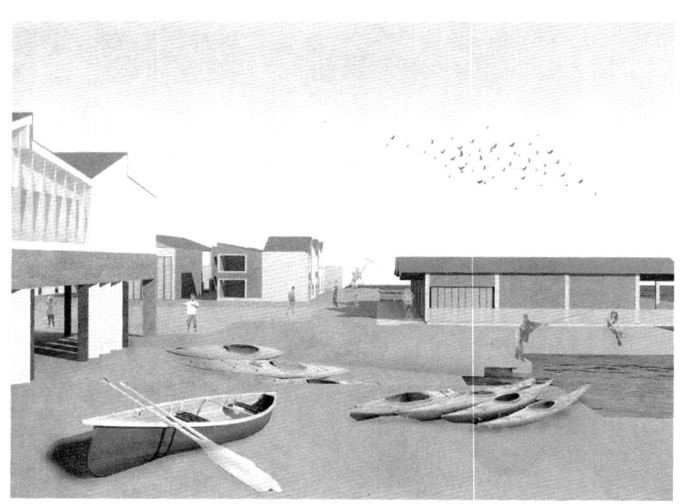

Exterior perspective view of the proposal, along the fondamenta and from the south lagoon.

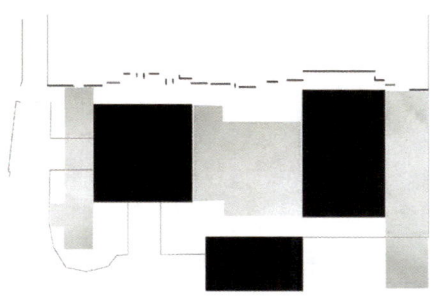

Existing buildings vs proposed buildings

Movement of garden into the site

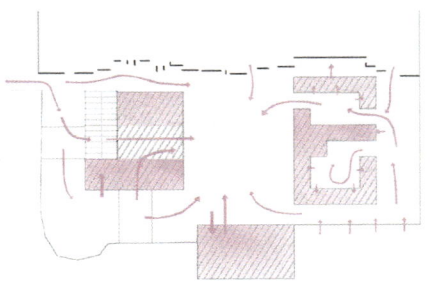

Circulation

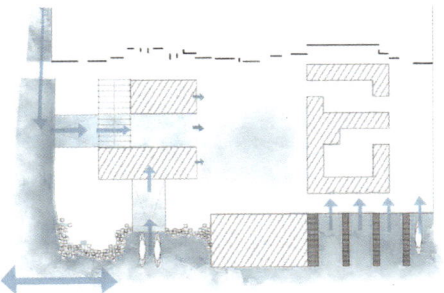

Movement of water through and around site

Exterior perspective
views of the proposal
design

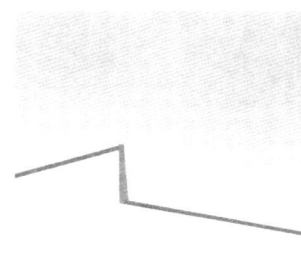

The North Front

The Workshop took place at Ca'Tron in Venice from November 22th to December 2th, 2016.

PROFESSORS: Enrico Fontanari (IUAV), Paola Favaro (UNSW), James Weirick (UNSW).
Tutor: Valentina Tridello (IUAV)

STUDENTS: Sobia Ameen, Laura Andretta, Erin Arthur, Dimitri Azzarà, Anna Bonetto, Claudia Borgogno, Caterina Carpenè, Lan Anh Doh, Caterina Dubini, Miriam Elia, Valentina Fracca, Giulio Grienti, Alessia Grippo, Yunjing Guan, Nee Shuang Heng, Tina Kan, Amandeep Kaur, Manasi Kundap, Bowen Li, Luca Emilio Longo, Joanne Ly, Man Hin Ma, Sarah MacDonald, Amy McNicol, Angel Miu, Laura Ng, Lauren Pieren, Yi Ren, Fera Rexhina, Lauren Rutstein, Madeleine Stocker, Sik Wai Tam, Maria Timis, Federico Tommasoni, Yan Man Tong, Sadina Tursunovic, Selma Tursunovic, Carlos Veas, Hai Lan Wang, Yuchen Xia, Diana Yang, Kyar Nyo Yin, Sally Yuen, Eleonora Zudich.

"Fondamenta Nuove"

Laguna North

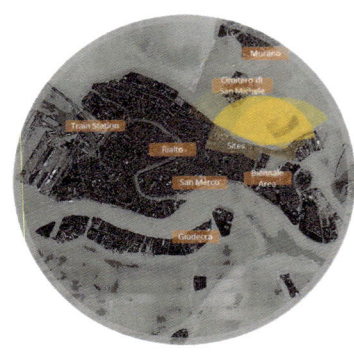
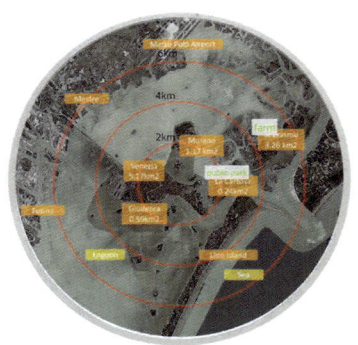
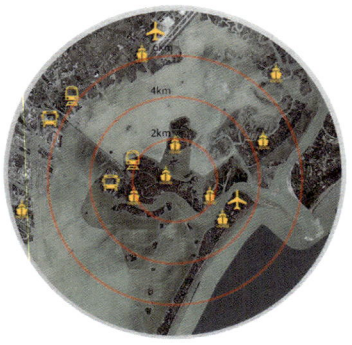

Bowen Li
Dimitri Azzarà
Luca Emilio Longo
Yuchen Xia

Existing function map

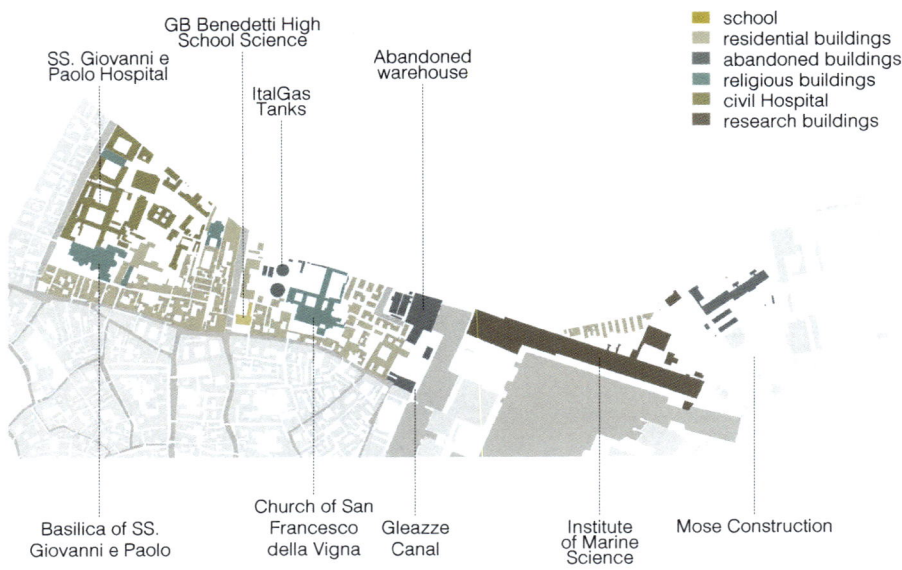

CITIES CANNOT GROW AND THRIVE WITHOUT PEOPLE - *what do citizens want in their cities?* Ey entrepreneur of the year (2016).

Our project aims to increase the wellbeing of Venetians. We seek to understand the emotional connections between the residents and the city, their happiness preferences, and characteristics that define Venice with local inputs. We focused on revitalising the community into a smart, sustainable city that resides over decades. Housing affordability, amenities, flexibility, and public space are identified as our main focus. Along with this, the possibilities, constrains, and potential development of each site were evaluated. The proposed vision was later allocated to bring in changes and to revitalise this site altogether. Based on our findings, our ideas were input to assist designers from other groups to address problems. By providing solutions, here, we maintained the integrity of the initial ideas of improving the Venetians' wellbeing, as well as preserving the valuable Venetian cultural and historical heritages.

Permeability and impermeability

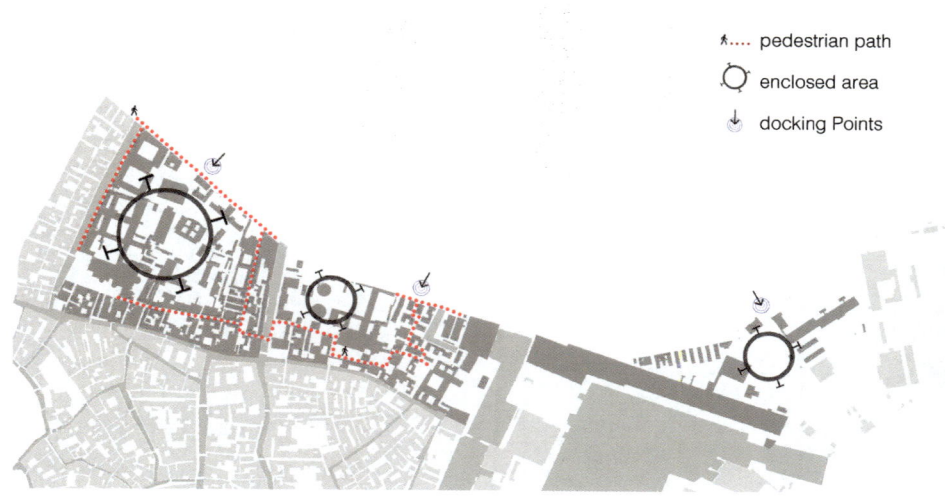

Existing accessibility

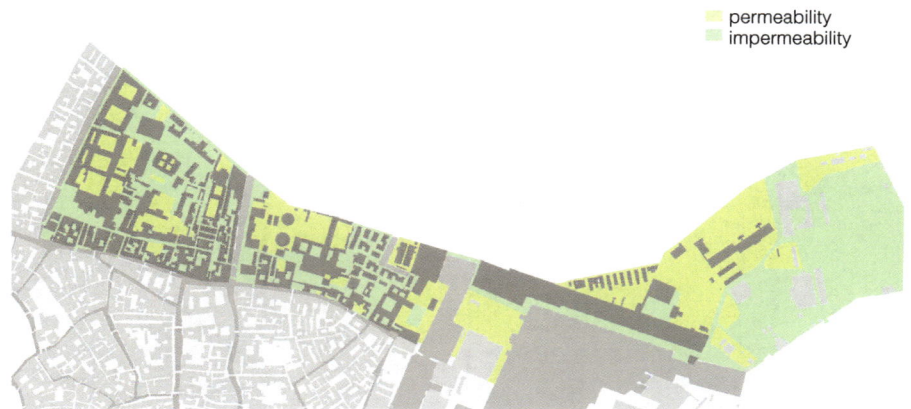

Main problem of the sites

Solution of the whole site

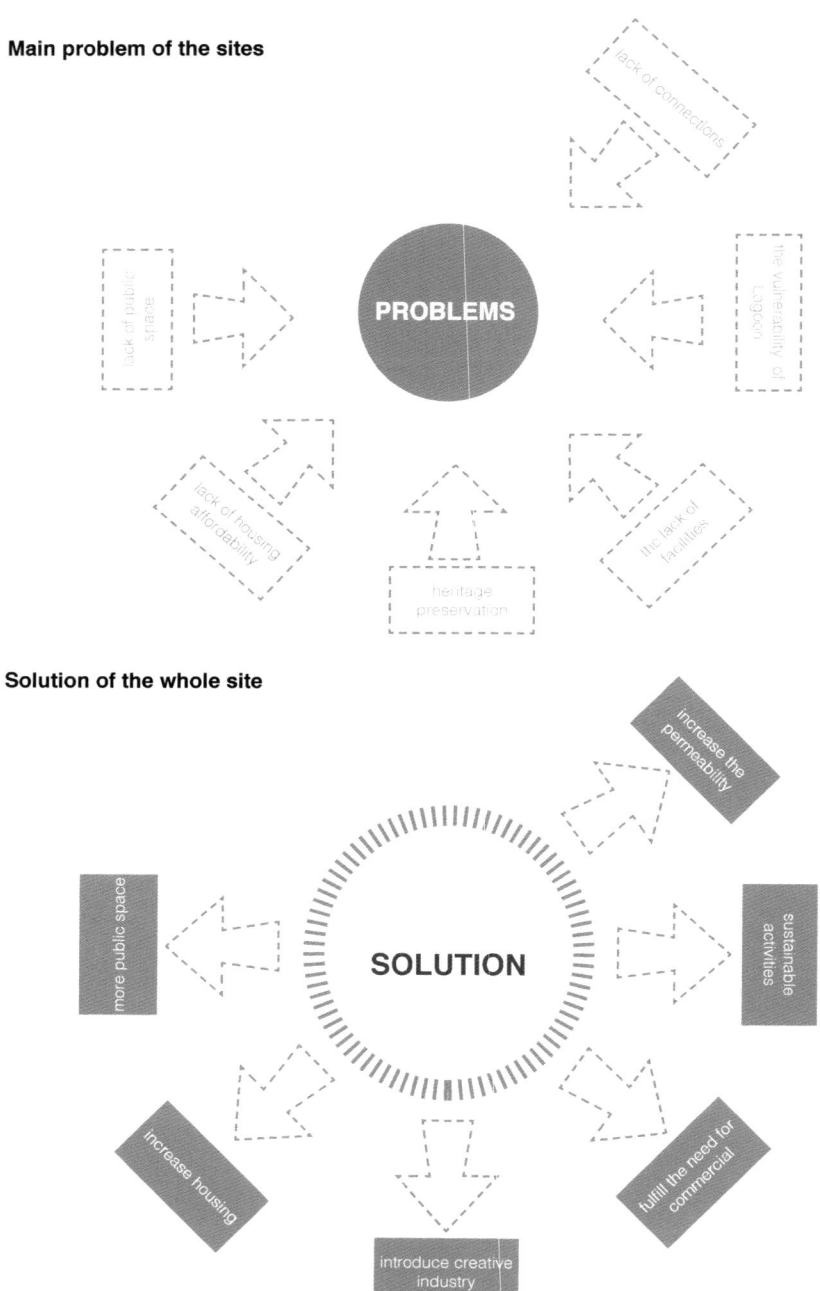

Project sites

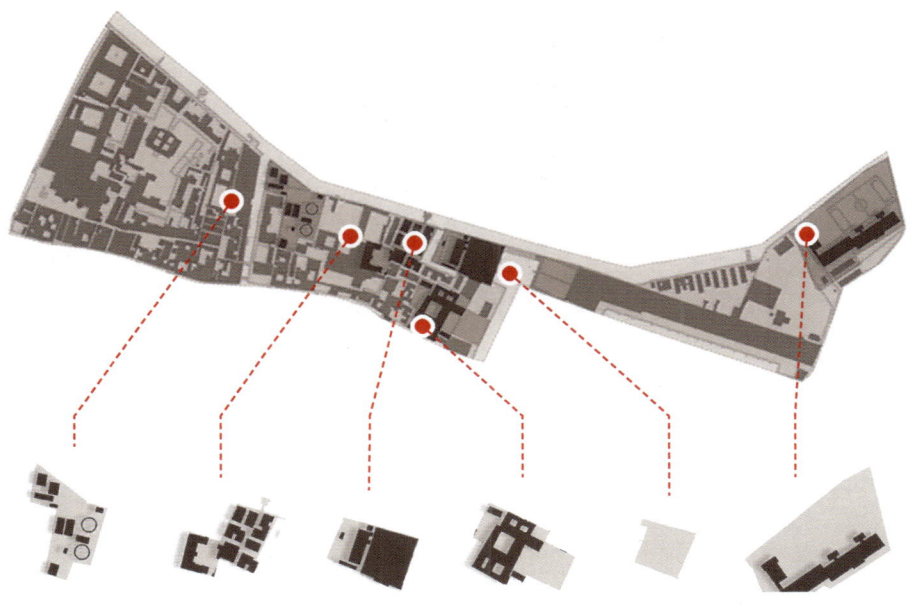

Gasometers
8245 m2

Celestia neighbotorhood
5782 m2

Galeazze west
7190 m2

Celestia's Archive
10365 m2

Galeazze east
4219 m2

Bacini's area
19985 m2

Allocation of the function

HOUSING   OPEN SPACE   RETAIL& MARKET   TRANSPORT   CREATIVE SPACE   LEISURE AREA

Proposed function

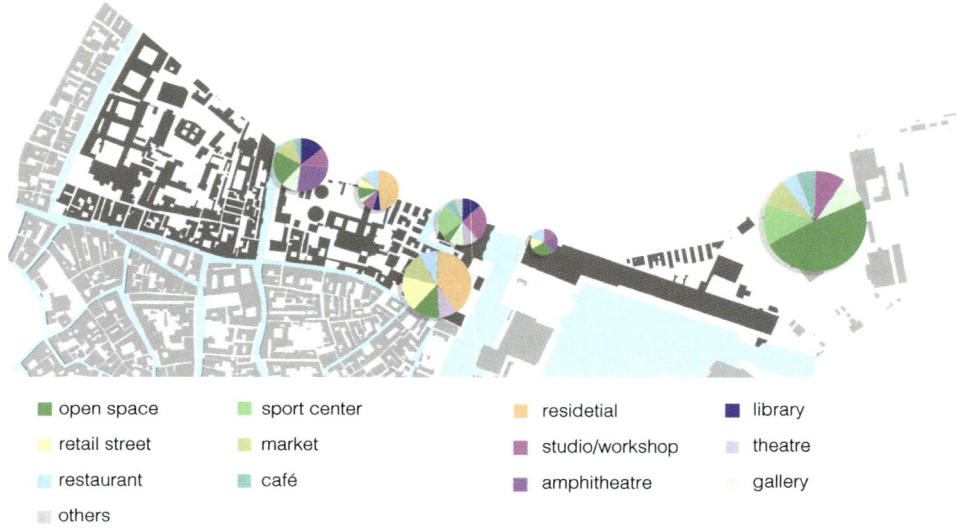

- open space
- retail street
- restaurant
- others
- sport center
- market
- café
- residetial
- studio/workshop
- amphitheatre
- library
- theatre
- gallery

Proposed routes design

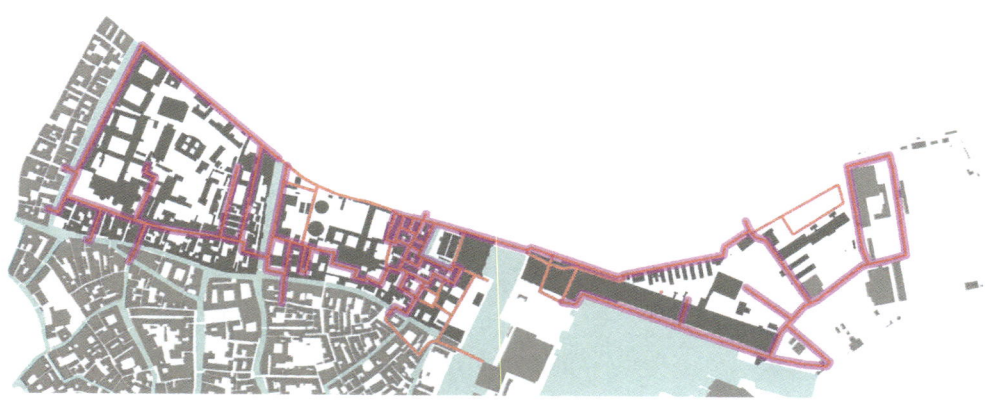

- new design route for pedestrain
- existing design route for pedestrain

New transportation structure

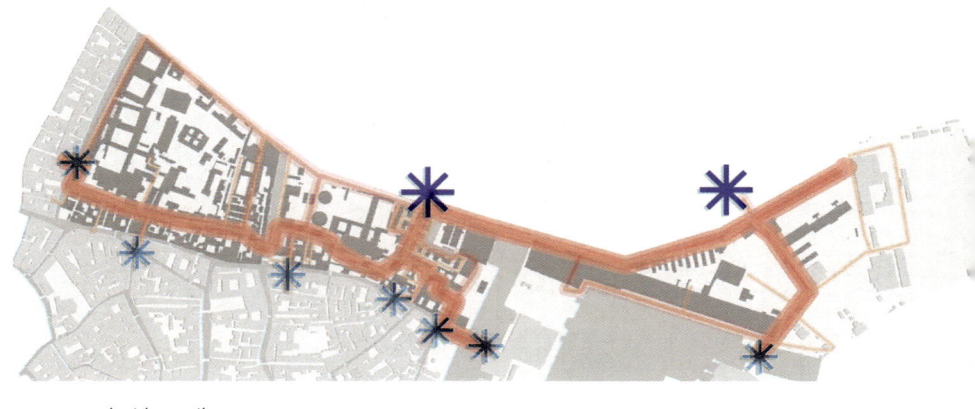

- pedestrian path
- main path
- * new pedestrian connections
- ✳ main water access

New transportation structure

- new public space
- existing public space

Santa Giustina Proposal
santa croce

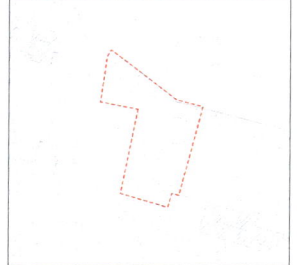

Site Boudary

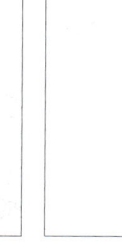

Flux filter

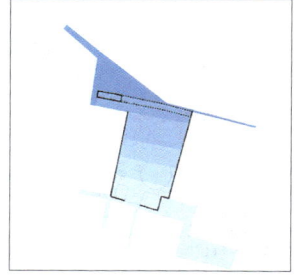

Pubblic/Private

Public (Darker) / Private (Lighter)
The nature of the site in regards to private/public and how it connects to other sites (Campo etc.)

Due to the site being primarily designed to cater to the community, the portico on the northern end was designed with in a porous nature that will control the number of people entering on site.

Federico Tomasoni

Joanne Ly

Sally Yuen

Man Hin Ma

Caterina Dubini

Miriam Elia

Erin Arthur

Masterplan

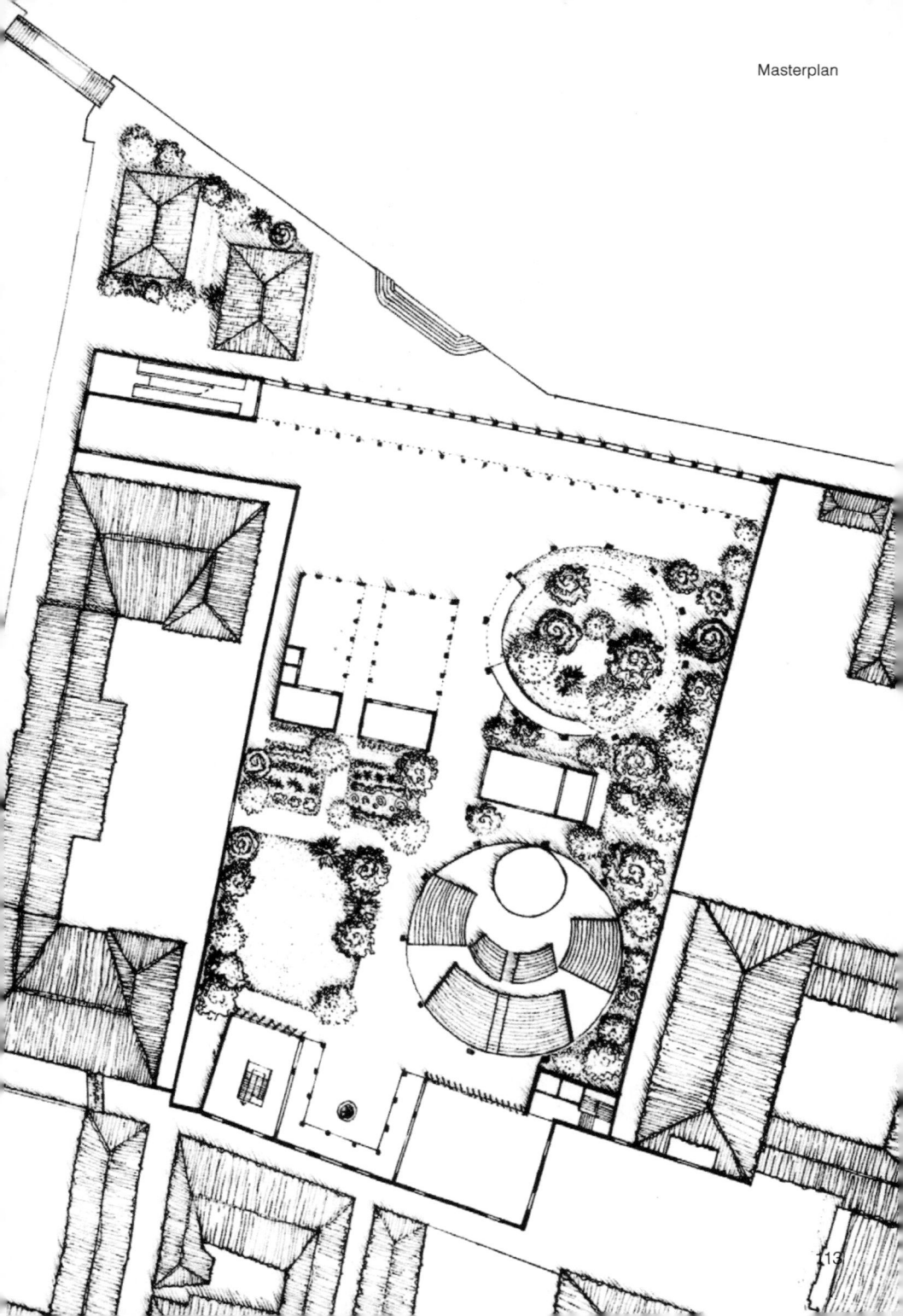

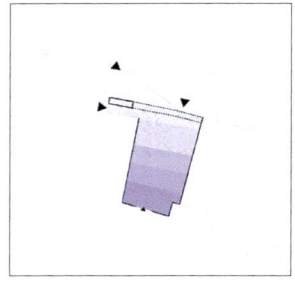  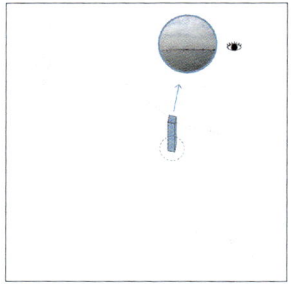

Point of entries
Circulation in relation of point of entry

Site Axis

View from the gasometer of the public garden

Bridging -Vaporetto-

Bridging the site and connecting it to Venice. Allows for the shipment of fresh produce from Santa Erasmo and fresh seafood from the lagoon, hence flexible markets.

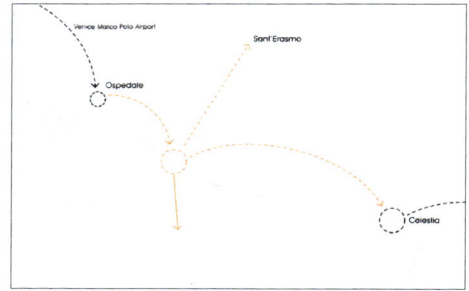

Demolitions vs additions

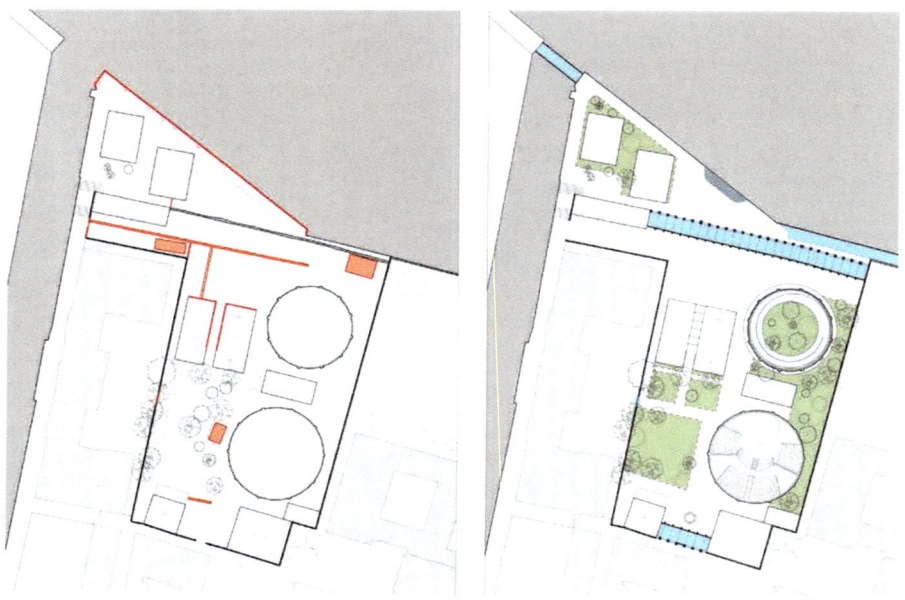

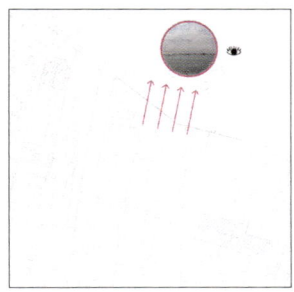  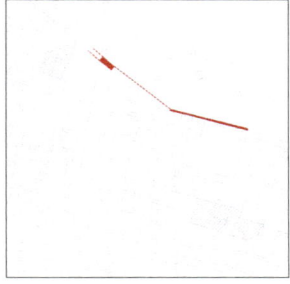

General View to Islands up North | Existing Vernacular as inspiration for the new portico (Flux filter) | Physical bridging and connecting it to the other sites.

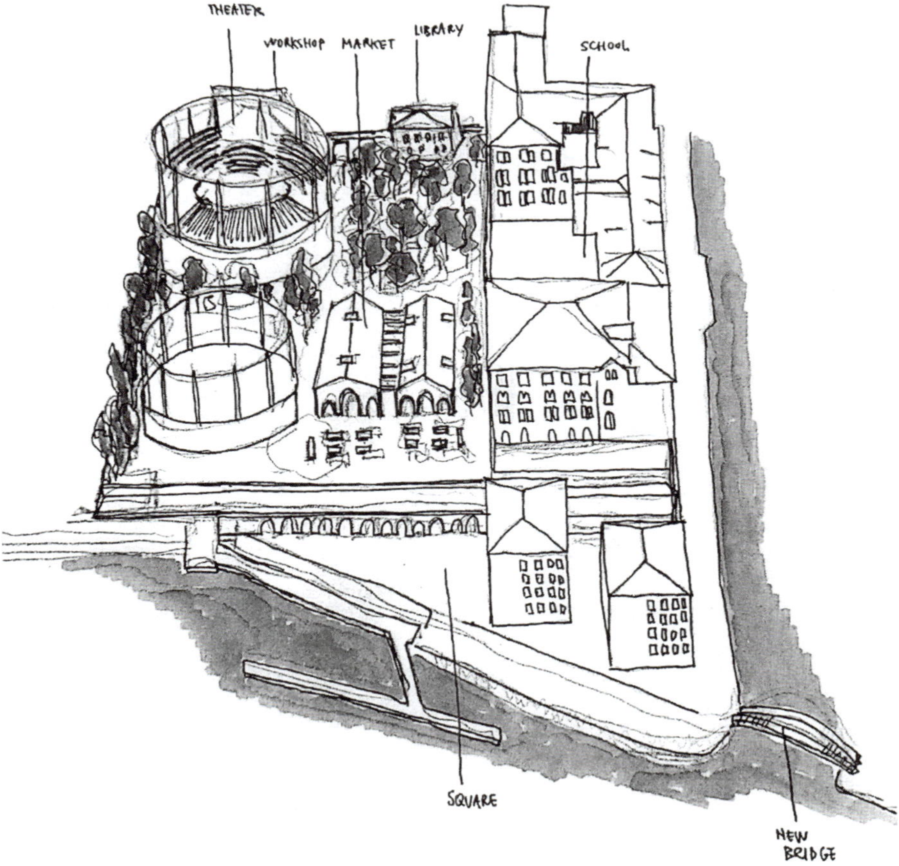

Sketch of the proposed functions

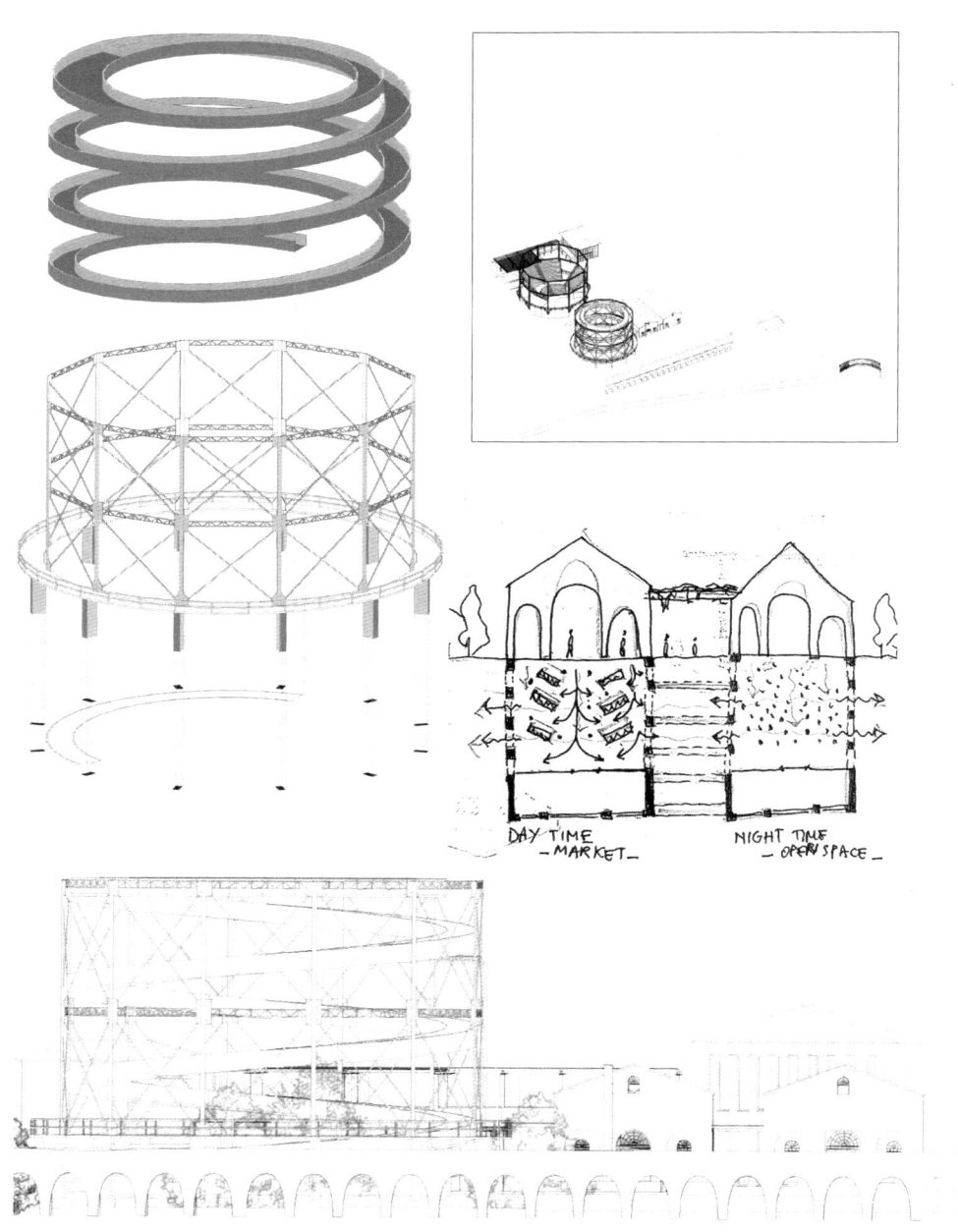

agoon Elevation

LEFT: Site Axonometric, exploded axonometric of greenhouse and sketch of the community market.

BELOW: Site's elevation from the lagoon

PREVIOUS PAGE: Sketch and exploded axono of the proposed portico facing the lagoon

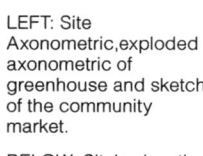

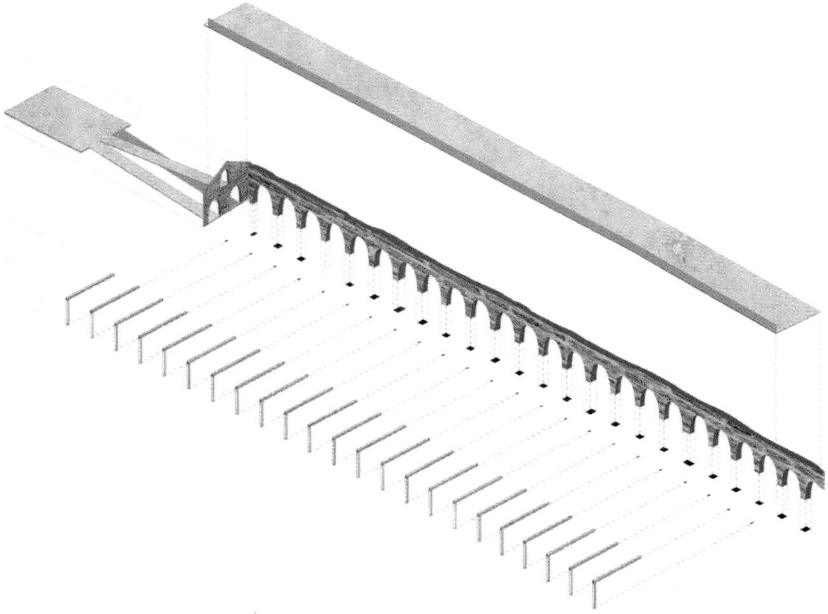

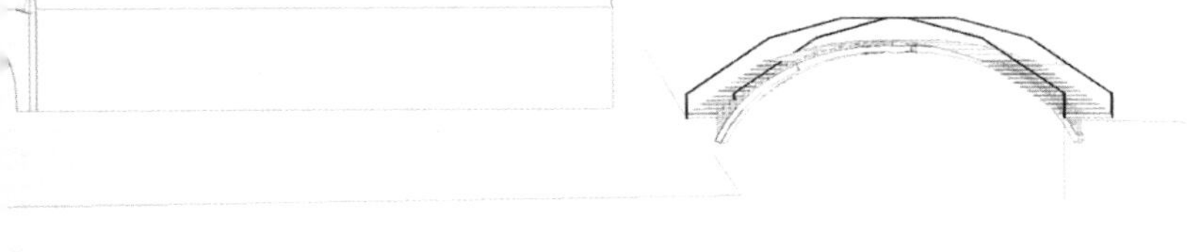

Due to the ever increasing tourism in venice, many residents have opted to leave the island. The aim of this urban renewal project is to reintroduce services that will serve the community rather than cater for the tourism industry.

The site is primarily covered in greenery to reintroduce the notion of public green spaces that will benefit the community as most of the green space in Venice is privatised. Services on site include a café, flexible market spaces, a function room, and two existing gasometers re-used as a public garden and an amphitheatre. These services were arranged based on a circulation study of the site, where the Northern half of the site is much exposed to the public use compared to the Southern side. The public garden within the gasometer, is positioned up north, and used as a public space. The amphitheatre is designed for community use.

Additionally, the market spaces are a response to the opportunity to ship fresh produce from Sant'Erasmo Island and fresh seafood from the lagoon. This is further established with a vaporetto stop in front of the site and a bridge designed in a familiar Venetian vernacular located on the northern west corner of the site essentially bridging and connecting the site as an embedded entity in relation to the other sites.

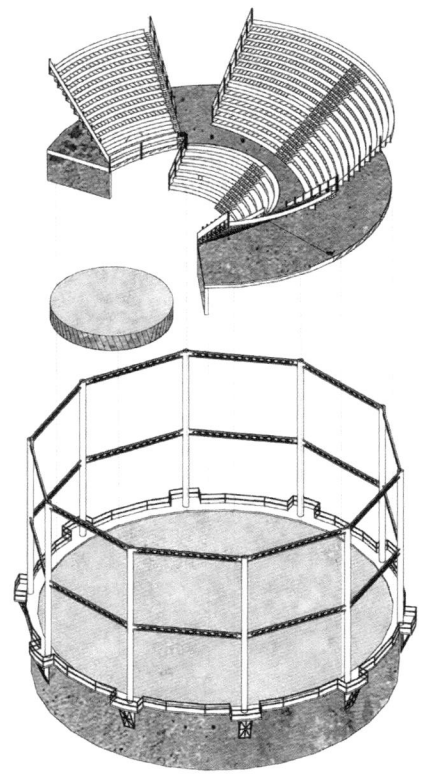

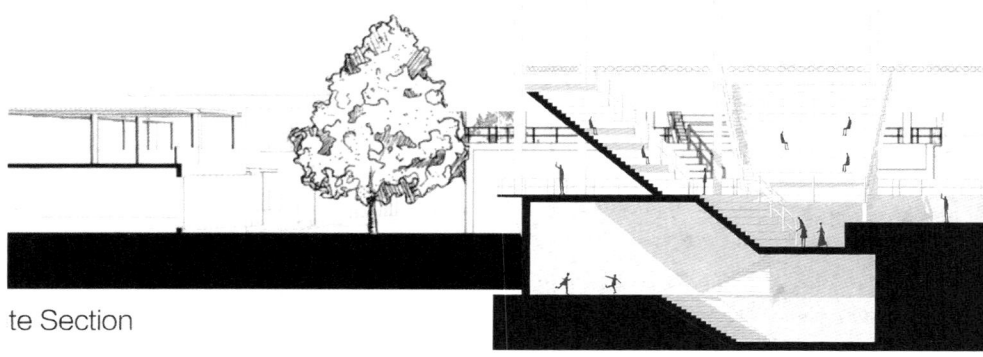

te Section

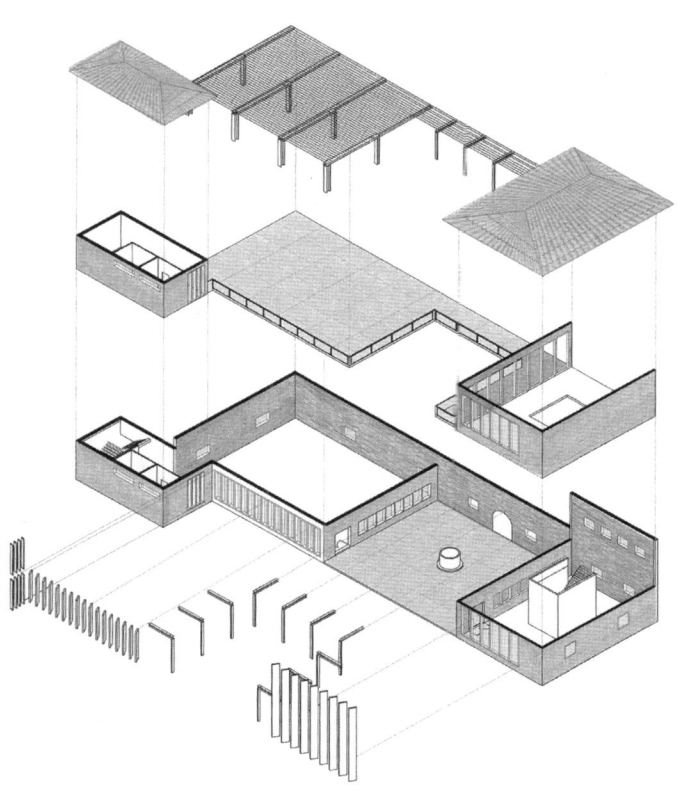

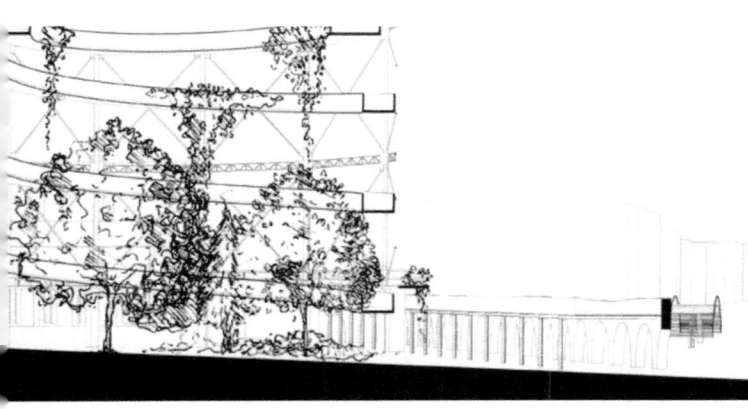

Exploded axonometric of the amphitheatre

Exploded axonometric of library and community center

Site section

Nexus
dorsoduro

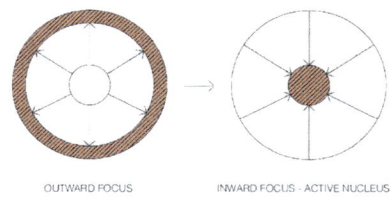

OUTWARD FOCUS   INWARD FOCUS - ACTIVE NUCLEUS

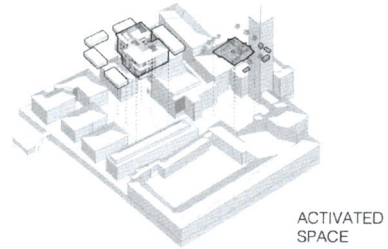

ACTIVATED SPACE

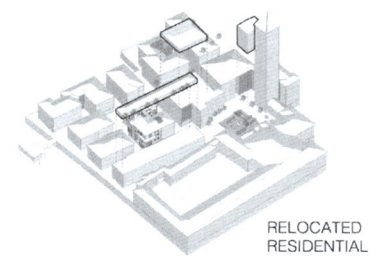

RELOCATED RESIDENTIAL

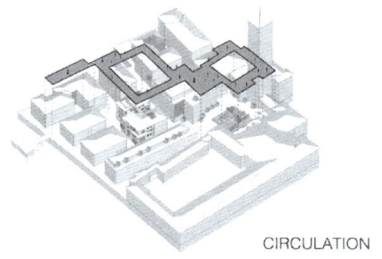

CIRCULATION

Carlos Veas
Sarah MacDonald
Maria Timis
Alessia Grippo
Lauren Rutstein
Diana Yang
Yunjing Guan

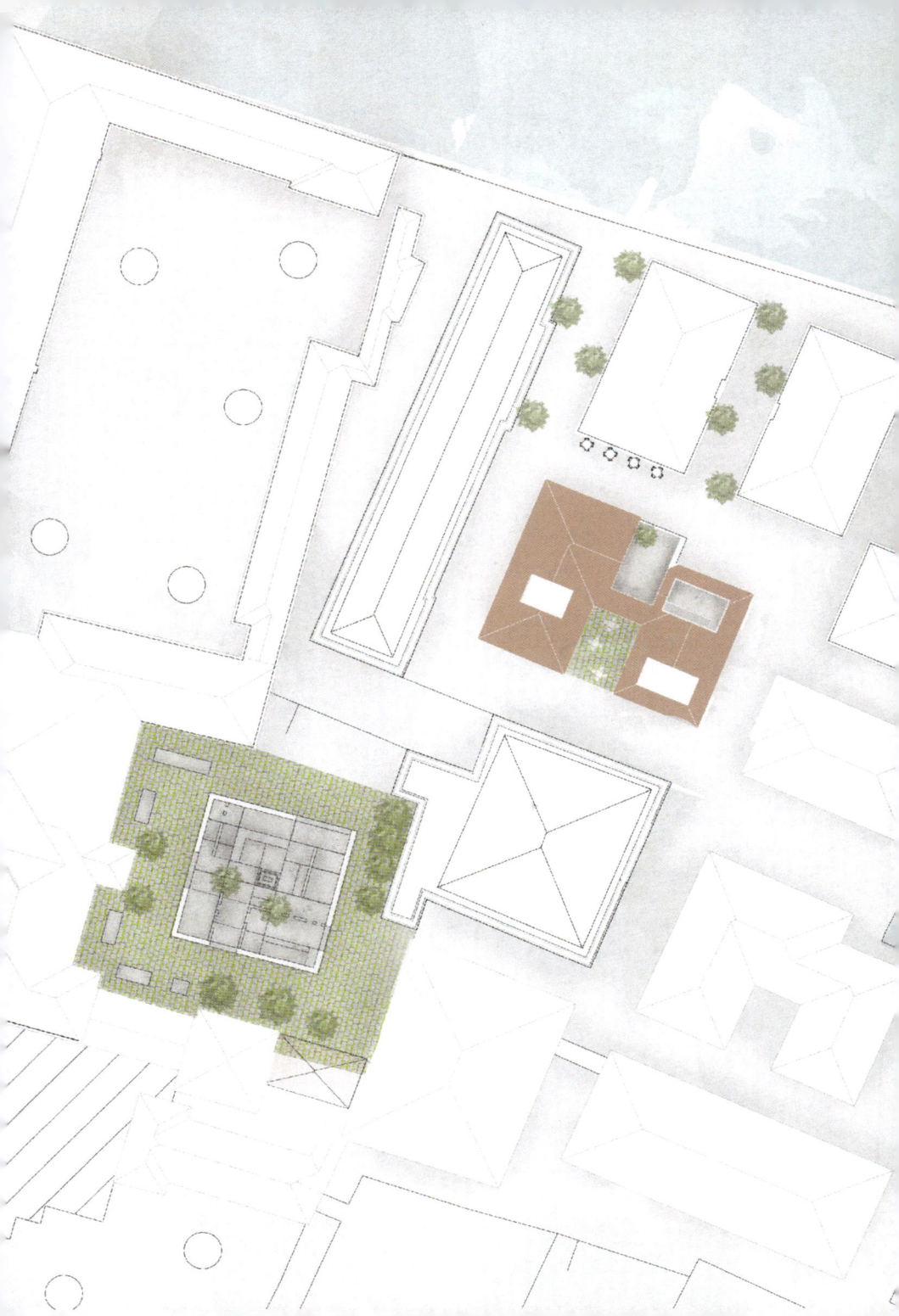

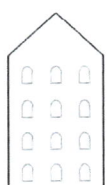 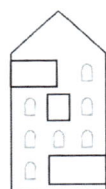 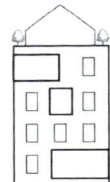

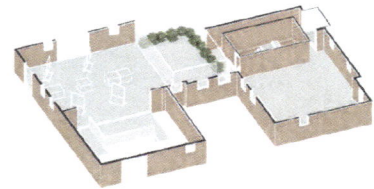

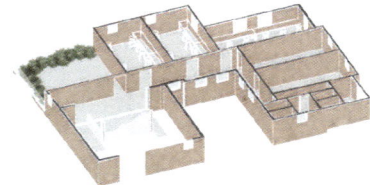

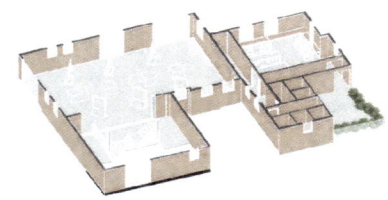

Aligned with the design of the Australian architect Harry Seidler, we aim to create a 'total environment', both experientially and physically, by developing an appropriate architecture utilising innovative technologies that reactivate the site to attract new residents. Nexus creates a central hub of activity that celebrates Venice's artistic and cultural past and future. This would include artist's studio or workshop spaces, exhibition spaces and outdoor gallery spaces to attract young creative artists and visitors. Furthermore, the design includes additional residential units and services for the community, such as a grocer, cafes, bars and restaurants, to enhance the wellbeing of the local residents. We propose to transform and renew the central building within the neighbourhood to create a nucleus of activity. We also propose to create better accessibility to the large open space and to intro- duce landscaping and architecture to establish a contemplative and re-ective public garden, to be used as an outdoor gallery or to suit the needs of the community.

TOP: Facade treatment, merging Old and new
COMMUNITY HUB EXPLODED AXONOMETRIC
4.Rooftop viewing platform
3.Gallery spaces, theatre and bookshop
2.Flexible studio, spaces and library
1.Gallery, workshops and casual seating
0.Grocer, cafe and foyer

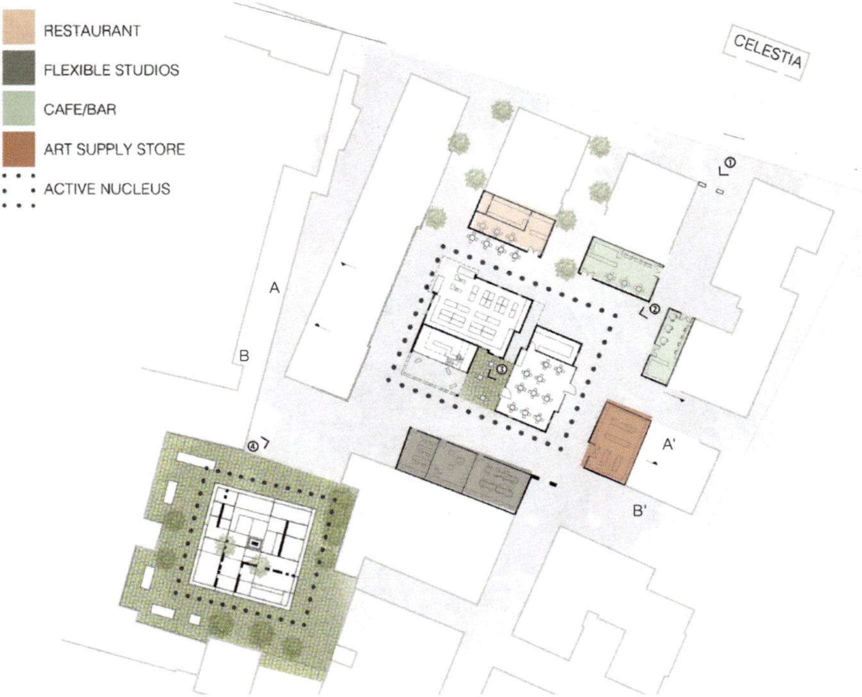

RESTAURANT
FLEXIBLE STUDIOS
CAFE/BAR
ART SUPPLY STORE
ACTIVE NUCLEUS
CELESTIA
A
B
A'
B'

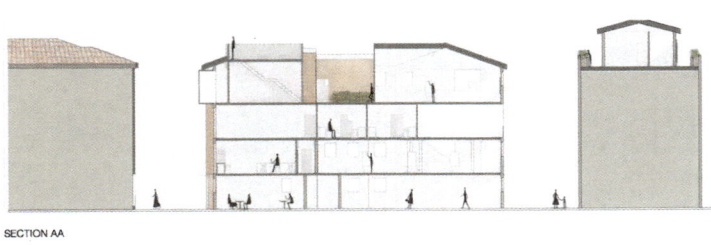

SECTION AA

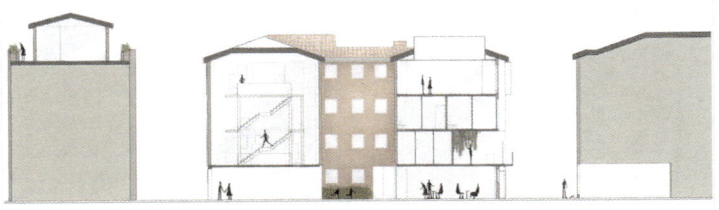

SECTION BB

Perspectives of the ground
floor of the community hub
Analysis of the materiality

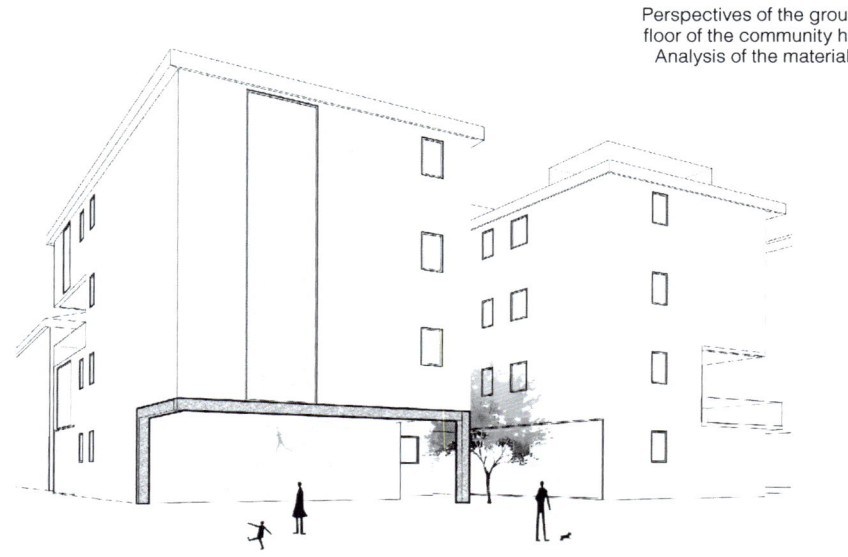

MATERIALITY - EXISTING

MATERIALITY - PROPOSED

1 - SUS-CON SUSTAINABLE CONCRETE
2 - RENDER TO MATCH EXISTING
3 - POLISHED CONCRETE
4 - GREENERY
5 - GLASS
6 - WHITE MATTE POWDER COATED STEEL

Groudfloor

First floor

Secon floor

Third floor

Outdoor sulpture gallery
design strategy and
atmospheric perspective

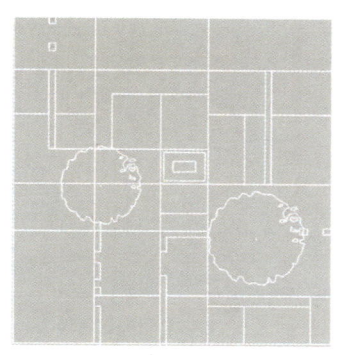
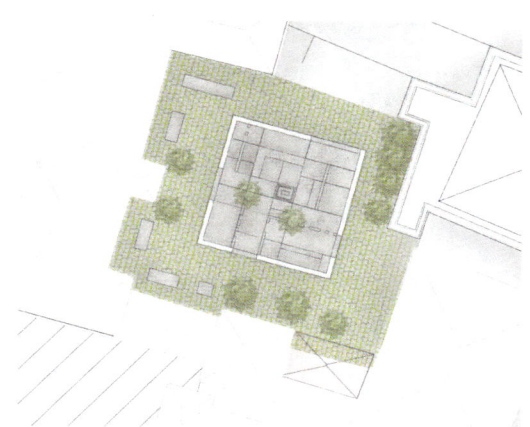

Cultural Revival
san polo

GROUND FLOOR

1. Public garden
2. Cafe
3. Boat learning workshop
4. Boat repair center
5. Rowing center
6. library
7. Restaurant

FIRST FLOOR

8. Green rooftop
9. Viewing point
10. Changing point
11. Office
12. Library

Yan Man Tong
Sik Wai Tam
Laura Andretta
Tina Kan
Yi Ren
Valentina Fracca

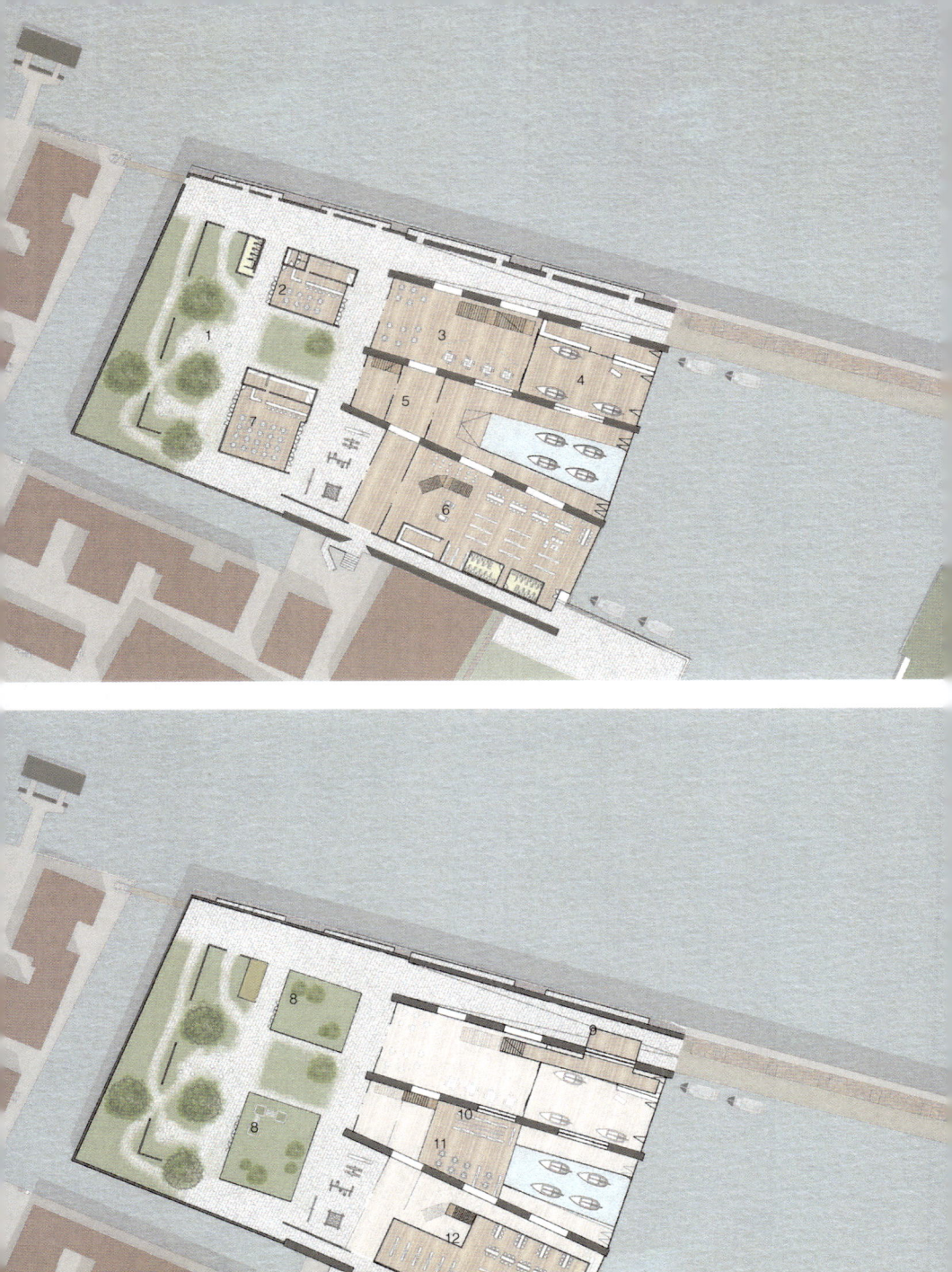

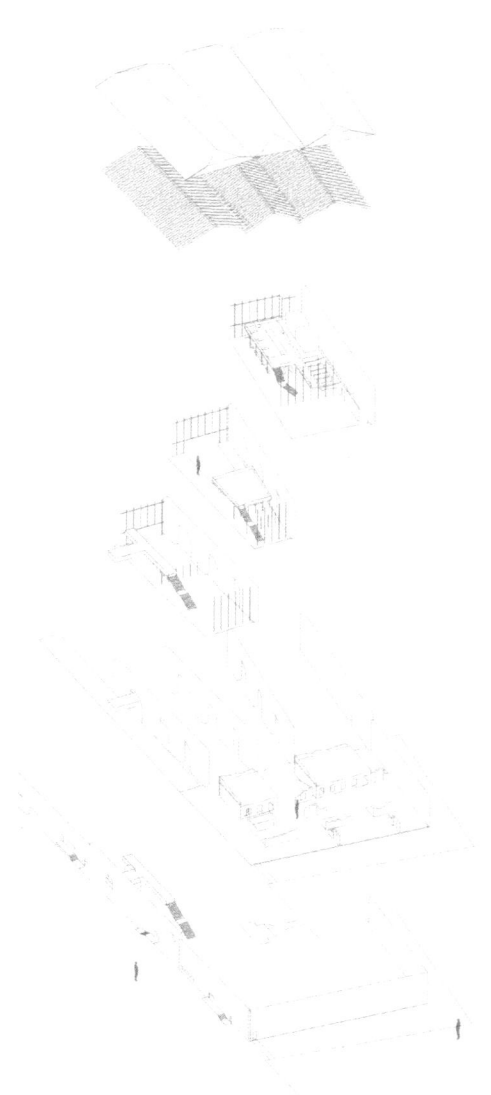

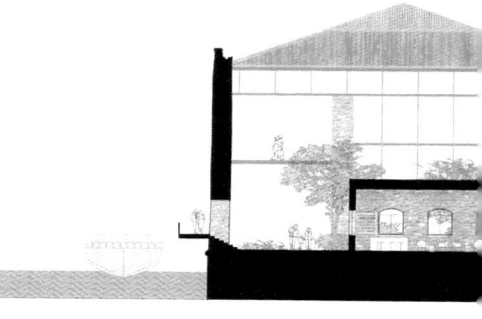

Exploded site axonometry

Representative collage from the public garden

Transversal site section

The galeazze west are situated in a working-class and non-tourist area. Major attractions and tourist terminals are far away from this residential zone.

Surroundings analysis

BIBLIOTECA SAN FRANCESCO DELLA VIGNA (LIBRARY)
• It stores data and news about the history of the building from the 13rd Century
• A reading room, some classrooms for the Institute of Ecumenical Studies
• Distance to the project site: 450m, 6min walk

CHURCH OF SAN FRANCESCO DELLA VIGNA
• It houses the Historical Archive of the City of Venice since 1826.

CAMPO DE POZZI
• Nearby: a bar, a children clothing store, a holiday apartment, and mainly surrounded by residential buildings
• No vegetation
• No public seating
• Approximate size: 410m2
• Distance to the project site: 550m, 7 minutes' walk

CAMPO DE LA CELESTIA
• Nearby: a university (Lab for Environmental Sciences), and mainly surrounded by residential buildings
• 3 trees
• 3 benches that can t 6-9 person
• Approximate size: 770m2
• Distance to the project site: 300m, 4 minutes' walk

Galeazze existing conditions
• Half occupied by buildings, half open
• Strong/close connection between the building and water
• Nice view to the water
• Large enclosed space
• Adjacent to a residential area

RIGHT: Collage of the new entrance to the public garden.

TOP: View of the public garden and of the new openings in the Arsenale's wall.

BELOW: Elevation from the lagoon.

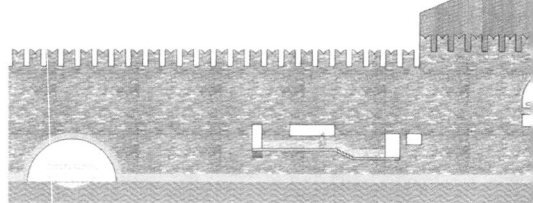

CALLE FRA' PIETRO
D' ASSISI

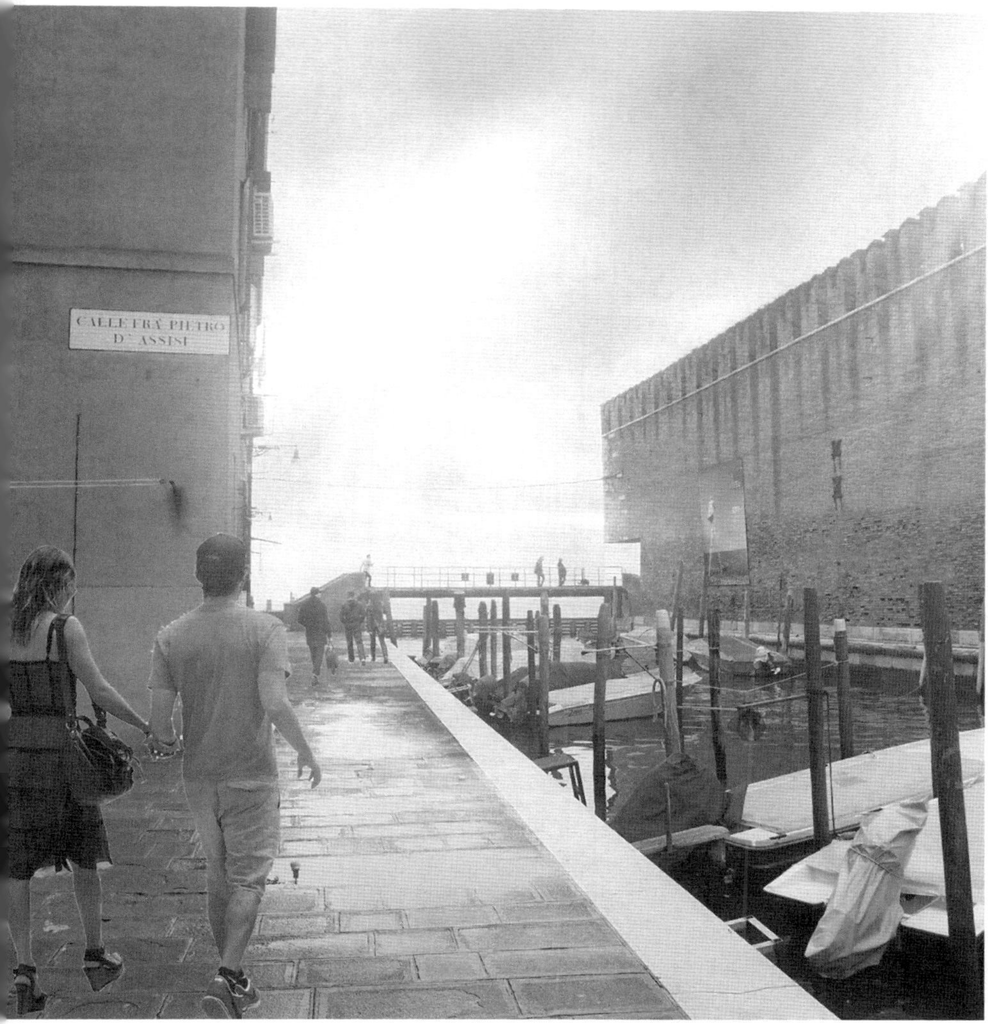

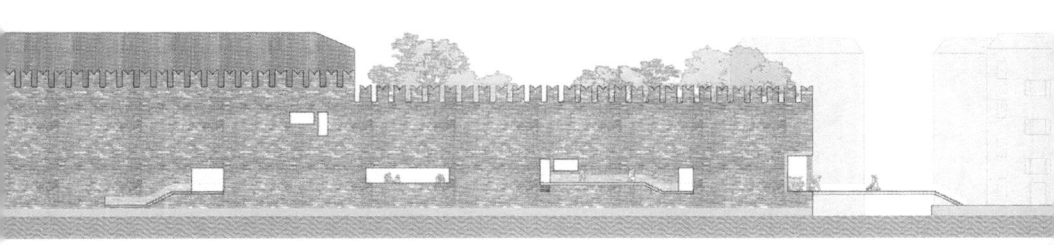

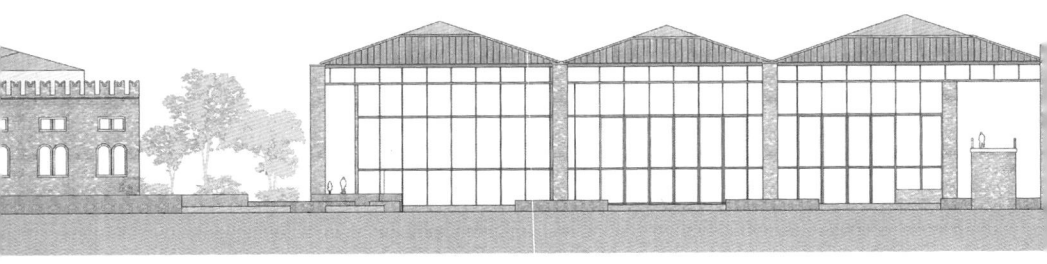

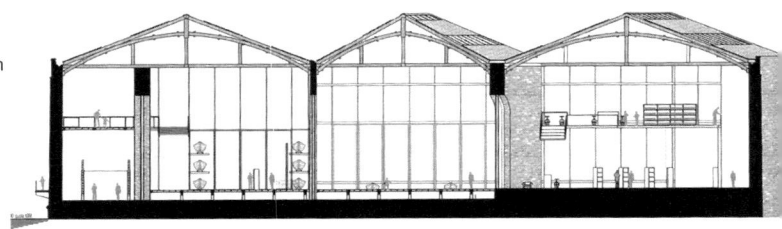

TOP: East site elevation
THIS PAGE:
Transversal section

Local voice
- "Jobs have disappeared to the mainland and tourists now outnumber residents."
- *Who can stop the slow death of Venice* by Tom Kington (The Guardian, Feb 2009)
- "Venice, as a lived-in city, is dying. A population which peaked at 164,000 in 1931 is now hovering at around 60,000. Since about 20 million tourists pour in each year - 55,000 a day - it's a safe bet that most days there are now more tourists than locals in Venice."
- (Kington)
- "Our cultural identity is at risk of dissolving if Venice becomes a theme park - we Venetians will not surrender!" - Local resident

Therefore, the wellbeing of the local community is the main concern of our design approach.

Objective
Restoration of the existing residential area and improvement of cultural and social spaces for the local community and the surrounding neighbours.

Proposed intervention:
Community Hub.
- A space serves as a second 'living room' or a backyard to the adjacent residential area
- Act as an entrance to the art/exhibition area
- Aim to serve the local residents and community of sourroundings.

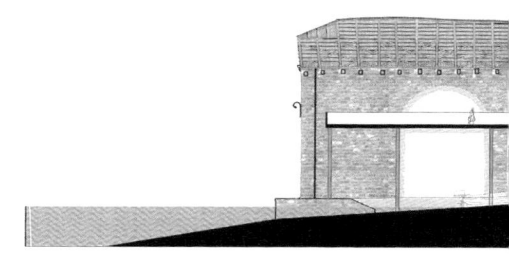

View of the library

BOTTOM: Logitudinal
site section

Campo Zero
cannaregio

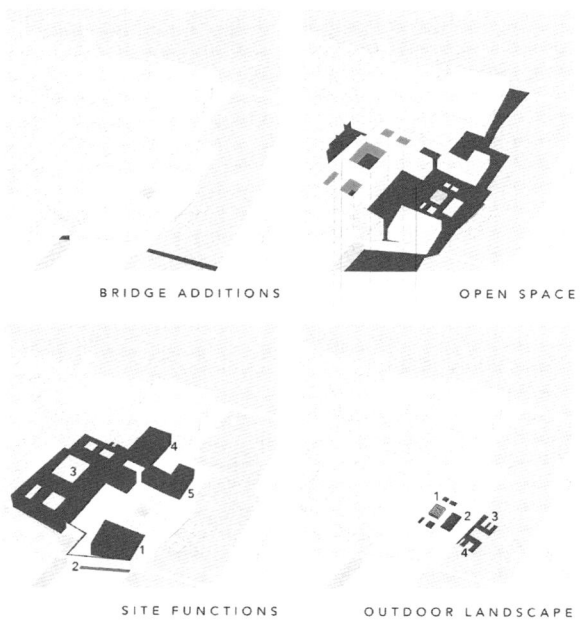

BRIDGE ADDITIONS
OPEN SPACE
SITE FUNCTIONS
OUTDOOR LANDSCAPE

Anna Bonetto
Laura Ng
Sadina Tursunovic
Zudich Eleonora
Sobia Ameen
Amy McNicol
Selma Tursunovic

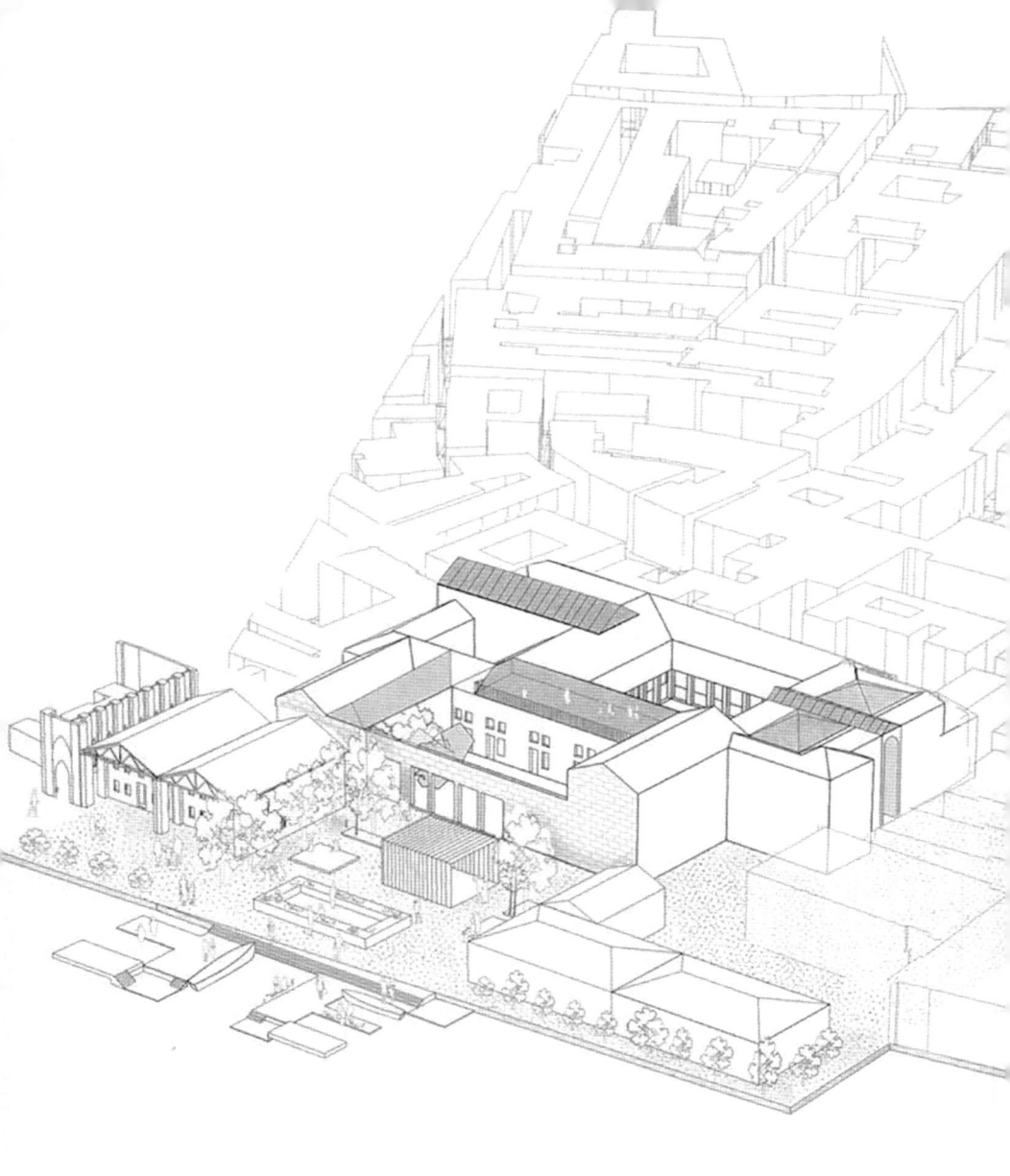
Bird eye view of the site

INSPIRED BY the manipulation of solid and void in Chipperfield's San Michele cemetery and the interplay of positive and negative space integral to the Venetian grid system, CAMPO ZERO seeks to create moments of pause and release. Embracing the unique morphology of Venice, the proposal explores the relationship between the water, land and its inhabitants.

This is expressed by re-establishing a connection between local citizens and agricultural products transported from islands less than a kilometre north. The land produce, water and people are brought into direct discourse at the proposed floating markets. Moreover, the design seeks to activate the existing buildings by inserting new residential, commercial and cultural theatre into the space. A relationship is created between the theatre, water and land through the inclusion of a water organ. This becomes an aural manifestation of the relationship between positive and negative space when it interacts with the natural processes of the lagoon context. This creates a theatrical exterior extension of our cultural theatre complex.

In terms of respecting the heritage of the site, our new insertions seek to leave a gap between the old and the new and to create differentiation through materiality.

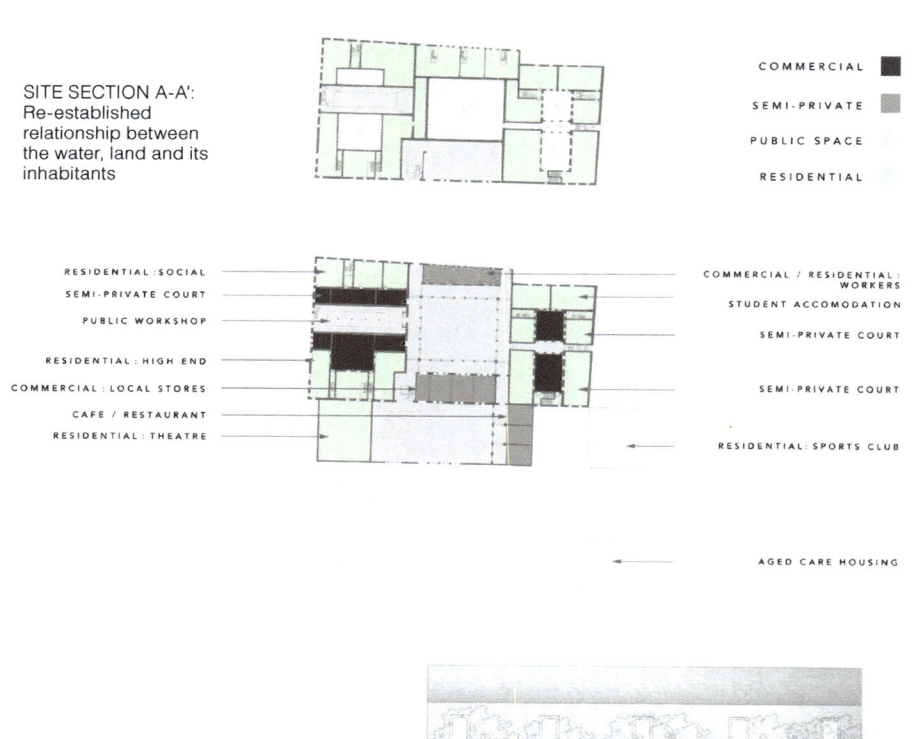

SITE SECTION A-A':
Re-established relationship between the water, land and its inhabitants

COMMERCIAL
SEMI-PRIVATE
PUBLIC SPACE
RESIDENTIAL

RESIDENTIAL : SOCIAL
SEMI-PRIVATE COURT
PUBLIC WORKSHOP
RESIDENTIAL : HIGH END
COMMERCIAL : LOCAL STORES
CAFE / RESTAURANT
RESIDENTIAL : THEATRE

COMMERCIAL / RESIDENTIAL : WORKERS
STUDENT ACCOMODATION
SEMI-PRIVATE COURT
SEMI-PRIVATE COURT
RESIDENTIAL : SPORTS CLUB

AGED CARE HOUSING

FLOOR PLAN

Apartments for 2 people	1
Apartments for 3 or 4 people	2
Housing for Theatre company	3
Art Gallery	4
Commercial	5
Apartments for 4 people	6
Apartments for 6 people	7
Housing for students	8
Pavilion	9
Water Organ	10
Market	11
Foyer	12
Theatre	13
Bar	14

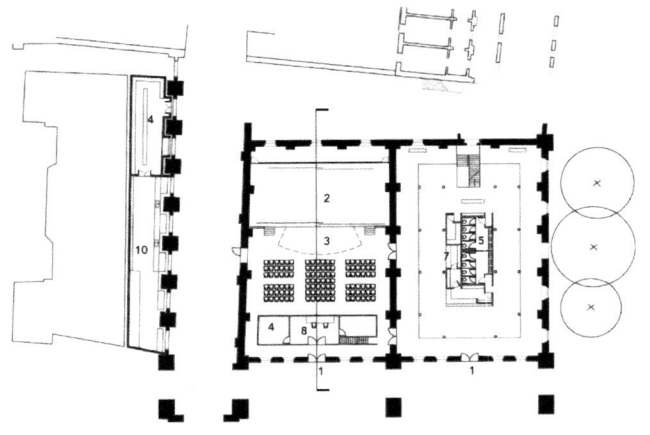

NEXT PAGE:
Exploration of solid and void   Longitudinal section of the theater

LEFT: GROUD FLOOR PLAN

1 Entry
2 Stage
3 Orchestra pit
4 Storeage
5 WC

FIRST FLOOR PLAN

6 Ticket office
7 Snack Bar
8 Studio
9 Backstage change room
10 Bar

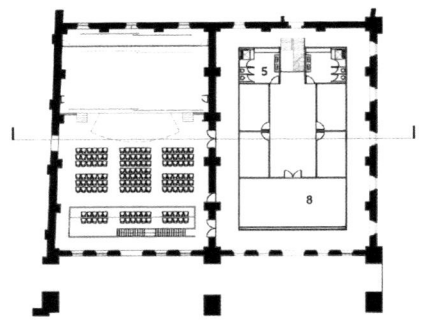

RIGHT: Transversal section
Highlighting the visual dialogue between the new + existing structures

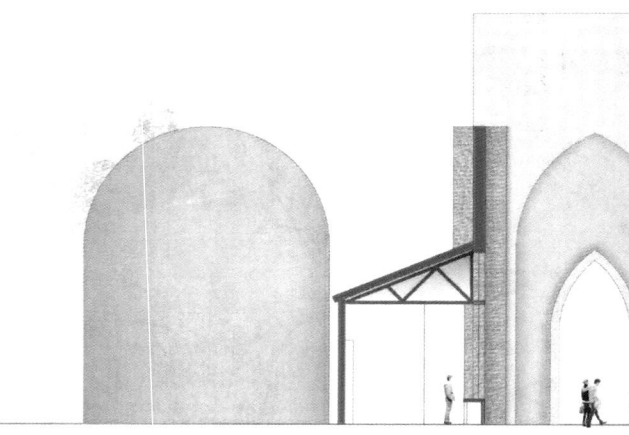

Negative   Positive

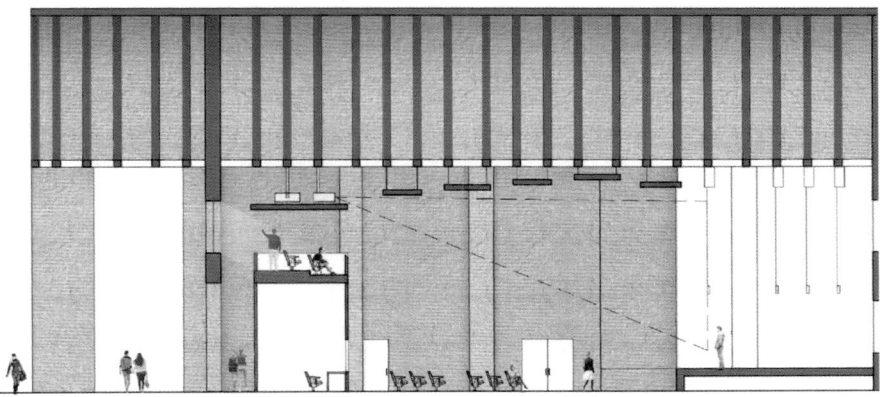

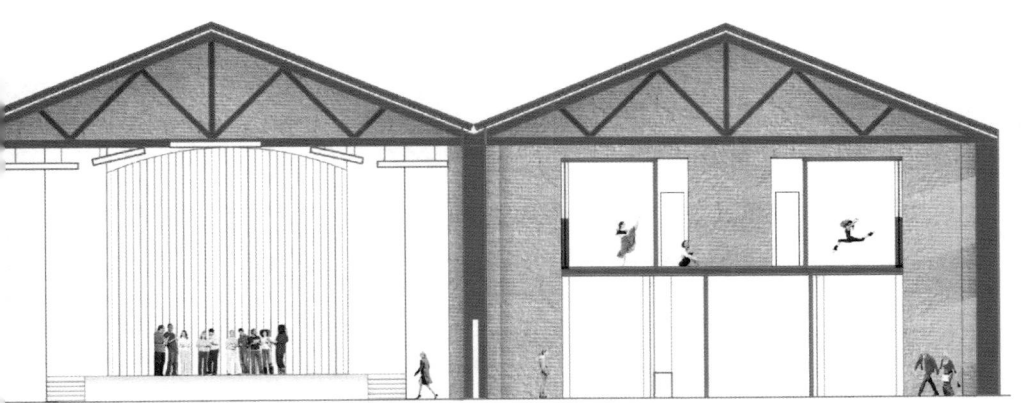

TOP: BAR ELEVATION
Existing entrance way in comparison with a modern interpretation

BELOW: Floating market

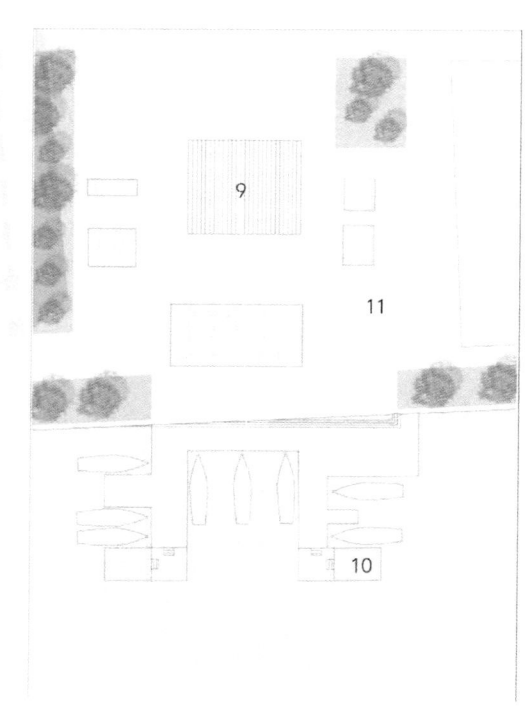

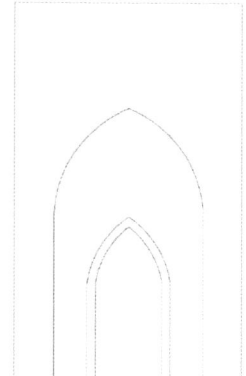

WATER ORGAN

An aural manifestation of the relationship between positive and negative space when it interacts with the natural processes of the lagoon context.

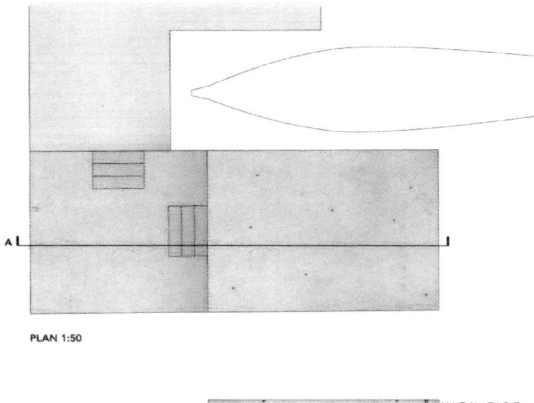

PLAN 1:50

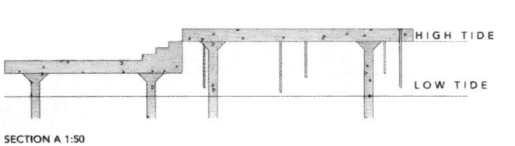

SECTION A 1:50

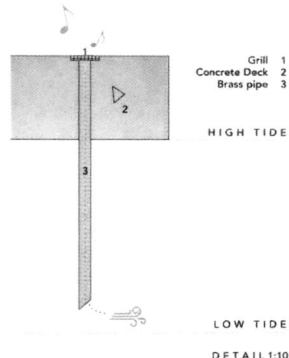

Grill 1
Concrete Deck 2
Brass pipe 3

DETAIL 1:10
Water Organ fixing in concrete slab

Interlace
san marco

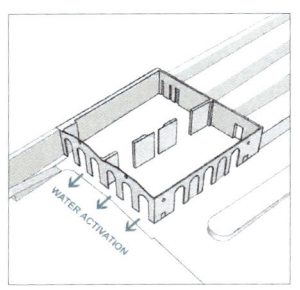 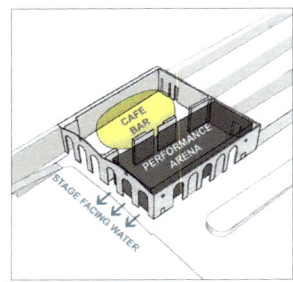 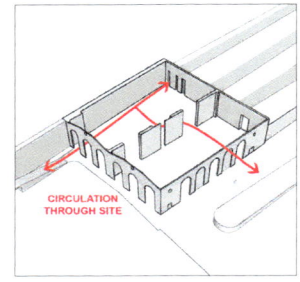

Madeleine Stocker
Fera Rexhina
Amandeep Kaur
Kyar NyoYin
Claudia Borgogno
Nee Shuang Heng

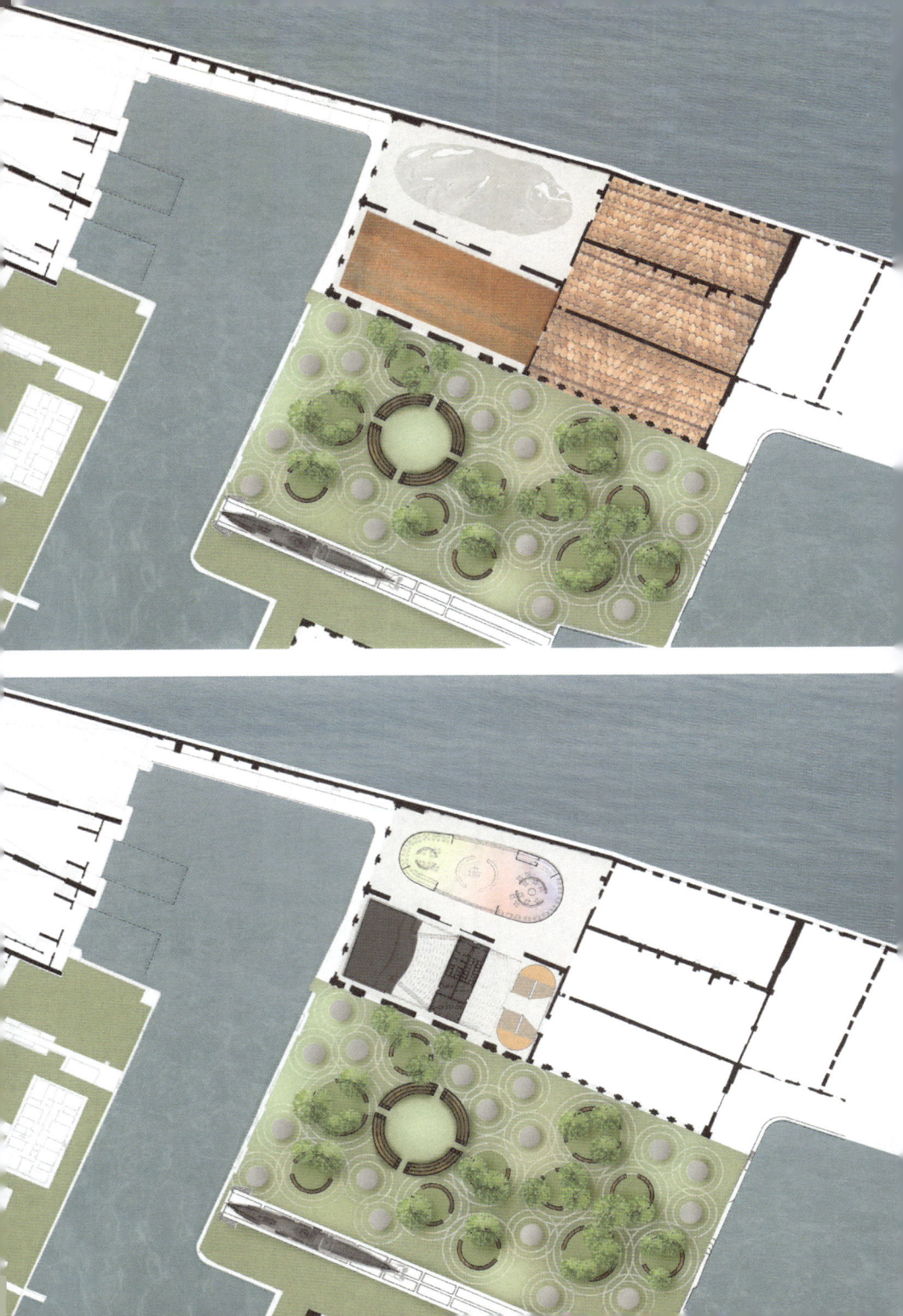

THE AIM OF THE DESIGN is to create a space for youngsters to enjoy performing arts, such as futuristic light shows because our site is surrounded by art programs like galleries and boat workshop. The theatre is in a rectangular corten steel box that changes colour as time passes by, becoming more noticeable as a new installation. It also opens out to the waterfront, interconnecting the performances to Venice's water. A café and bar for pre- and post-functional activities are in a contrasting irregular form in frosted plastic. It lights up colourfully at night, making it noticeable from outside of the high wall.

NEXT PAGE: Functional scheme

BELOW: Bird eye view of the proposal

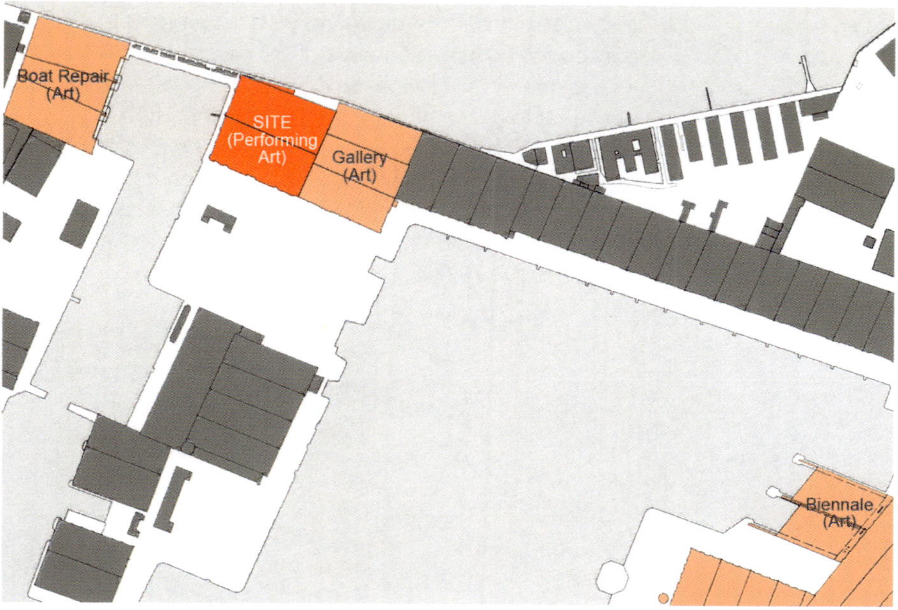
Boat Repair
(Art)
SITE
(Performing
Art)
Gallery
(Art)
Biennale
(Art)

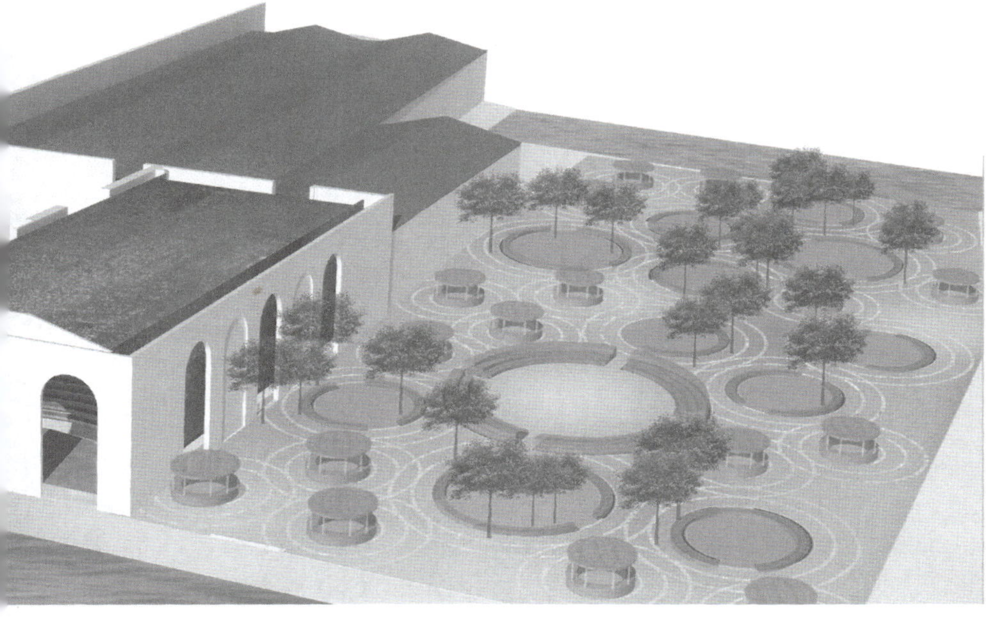

The café and bar are designed with a sunken public space in between to connect the users of the two spaces. Putting the functions into pods allowed for better public circulation around the building to get to other places and feel the fusion between the new forms and the old walls. The outdoor market follows the concept of pods and allow interaction between different socio-economic classes. It has a lot of open space compared to the claustrophobic market streets of Venice. The ripple patterns on the floor also alludes to Venice's water.

NEXT PAGE: Exploded axonometric of the bar strusture

BELOW: Section of the bar

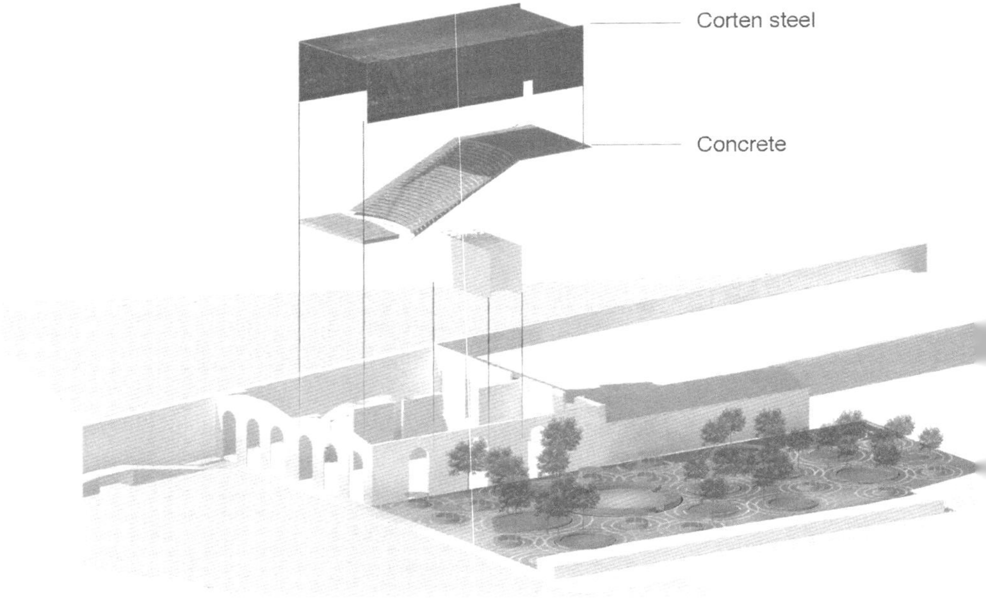

Corten steel

Concrete

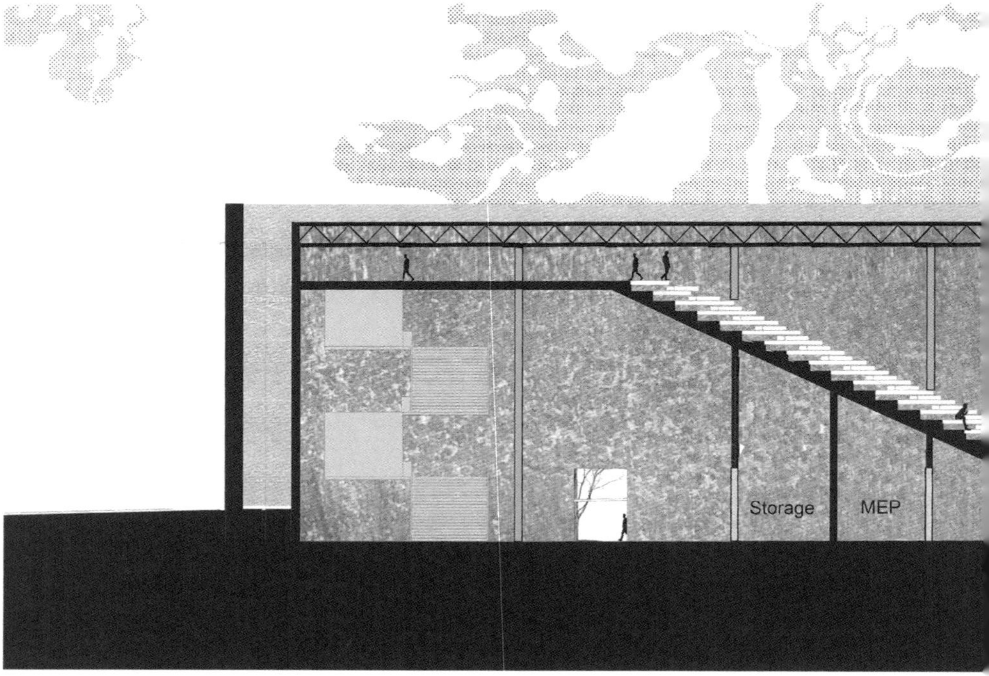

Storage | MEP

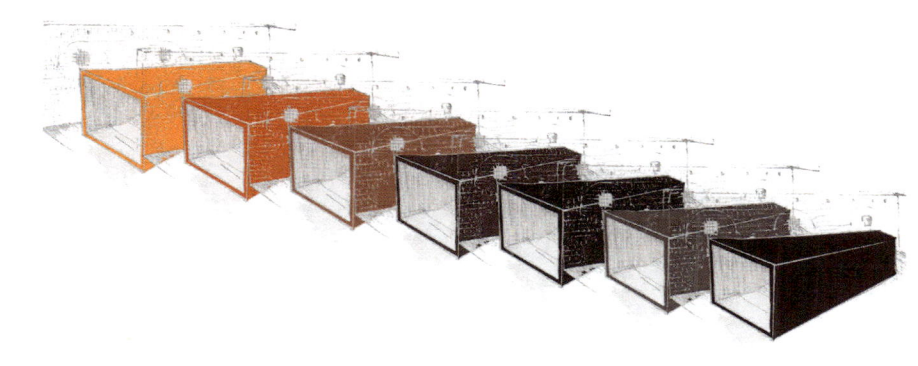

UP: Ageing process of corten steel

PREVIOUS PAGE: Exploded axonometric of the theater

BELOW: Section of the theater

Connections
castello

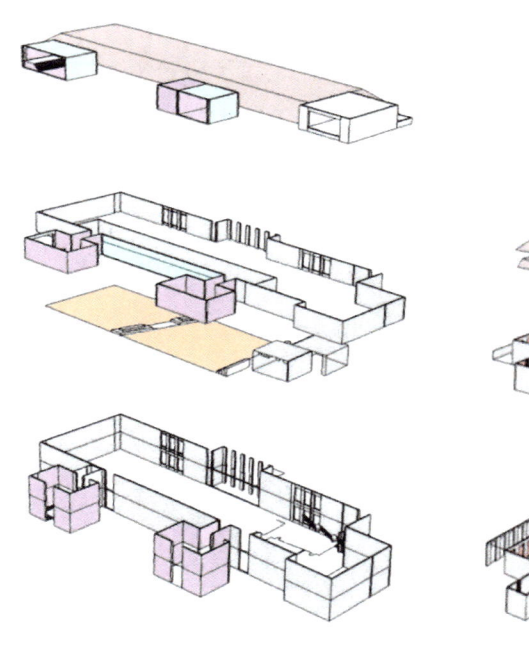
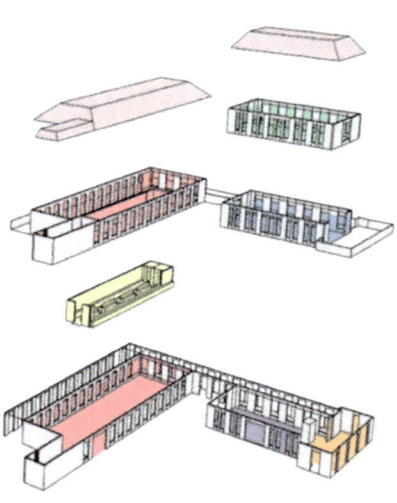

Hai Lan Wang
Laure Pieren
Caterina Carpenè
Lan Anh Doh
Angel Miu
Giulio Grienti
Manasi Kundap

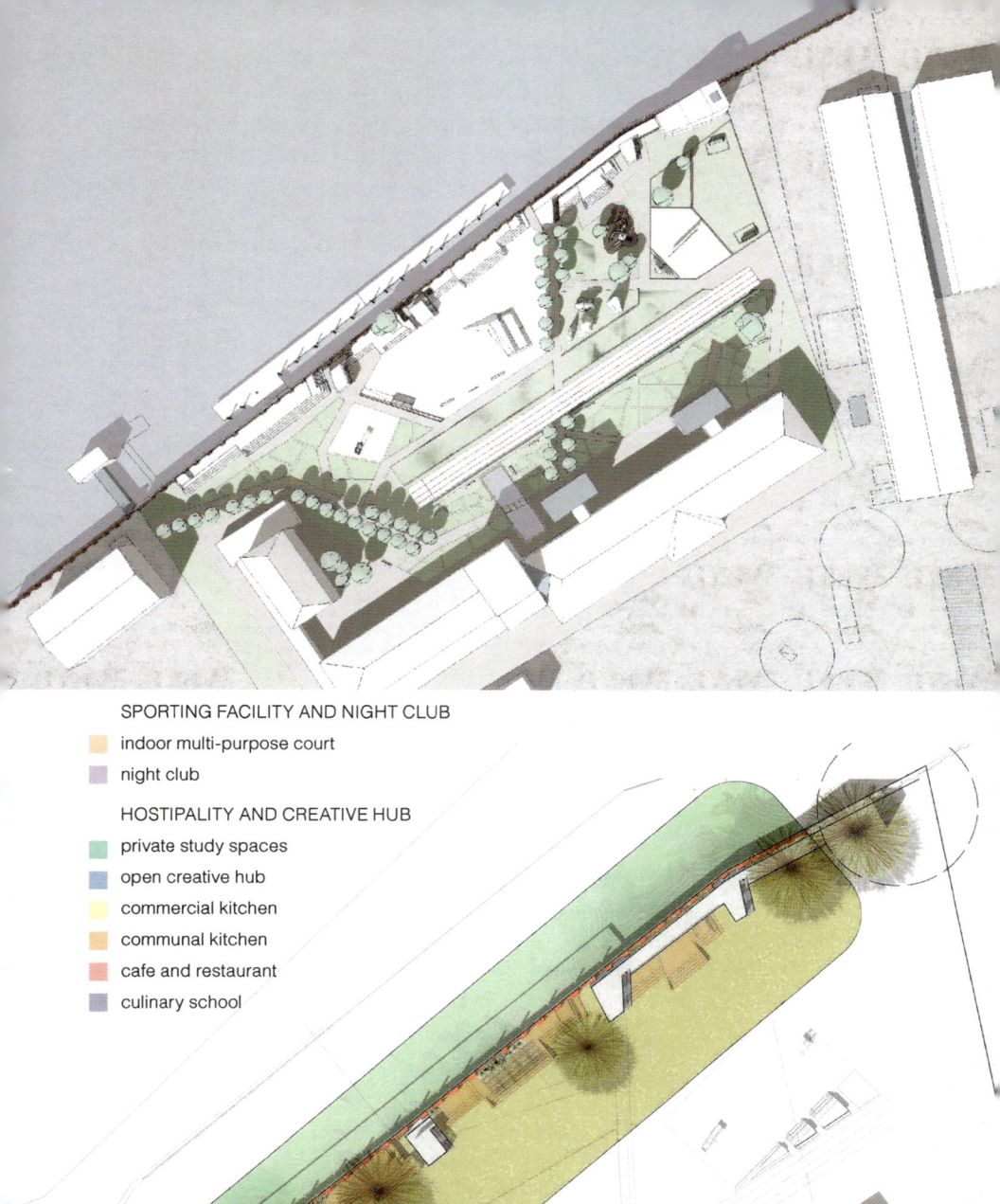

Section of the creative hub and study space

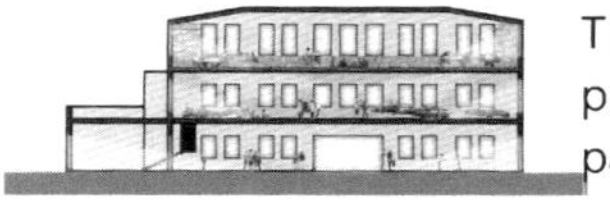

Recreational park.
The recreational park is designed to provide optimal facilities such as a skatepark, children's playground, multi-use sport courts, running track, bicycle trail and picnic areas for the locals to enjoy. Footpaths are carved in the landscape in relation to the direction of the islands Murano, Burano & surrounding islands.

Sports Centre:
Indoor sporting recreational space that provides multiple courts and a gym.

Aqua Alta:
The go-to night spot for Venice. It is a featured EDM night club with the vibrant atmosphere for the night owls.

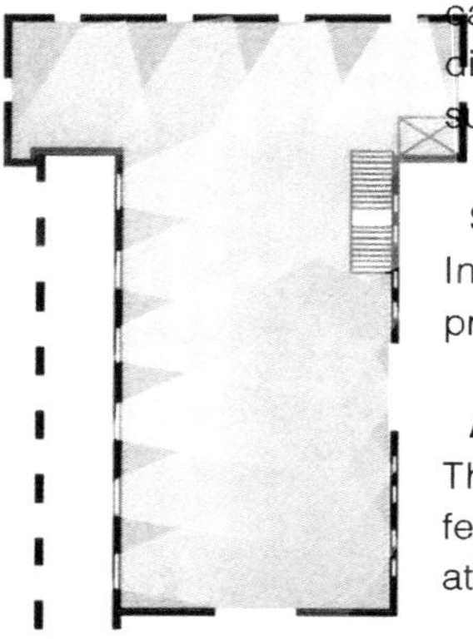

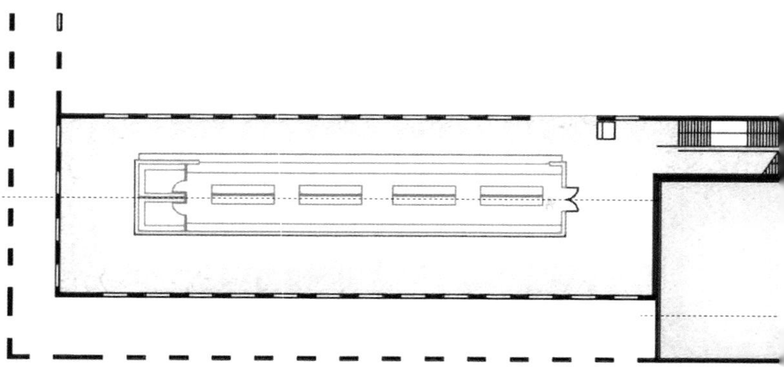

NEXT PAGE:
Section of the night club

Section of the gym and the restaurant

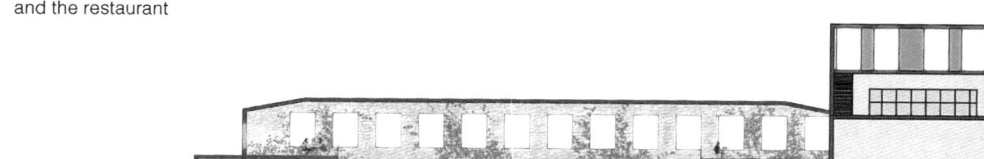

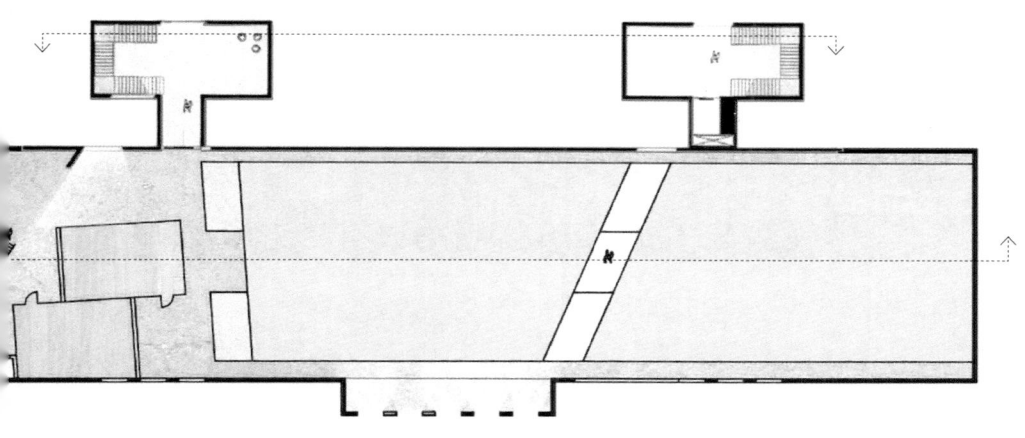
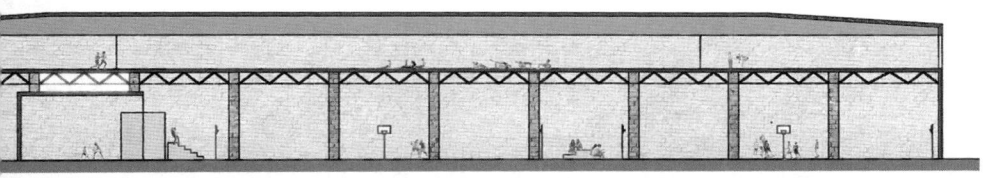

The Wall.

Incorporating the historic wall, a new constructed path is created to provide view of the islands. Mirador Is the last point of the pathway, where you can experience Venice from a new viewpoint. Surrounding this new form is a recreational space that is activated during day by families& children. The hub & sporting facilities promote fitness & creativity. The site is activated at night by facilitating a roof nightclub for the large student population in Venezia.

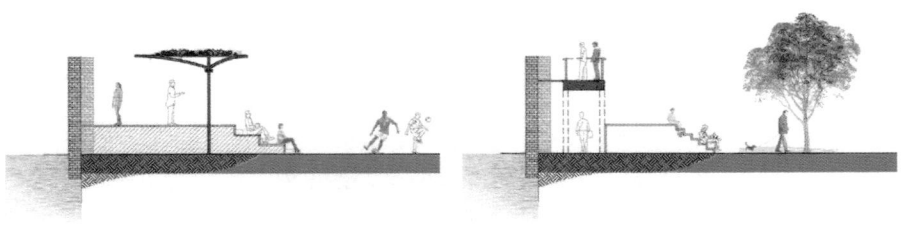

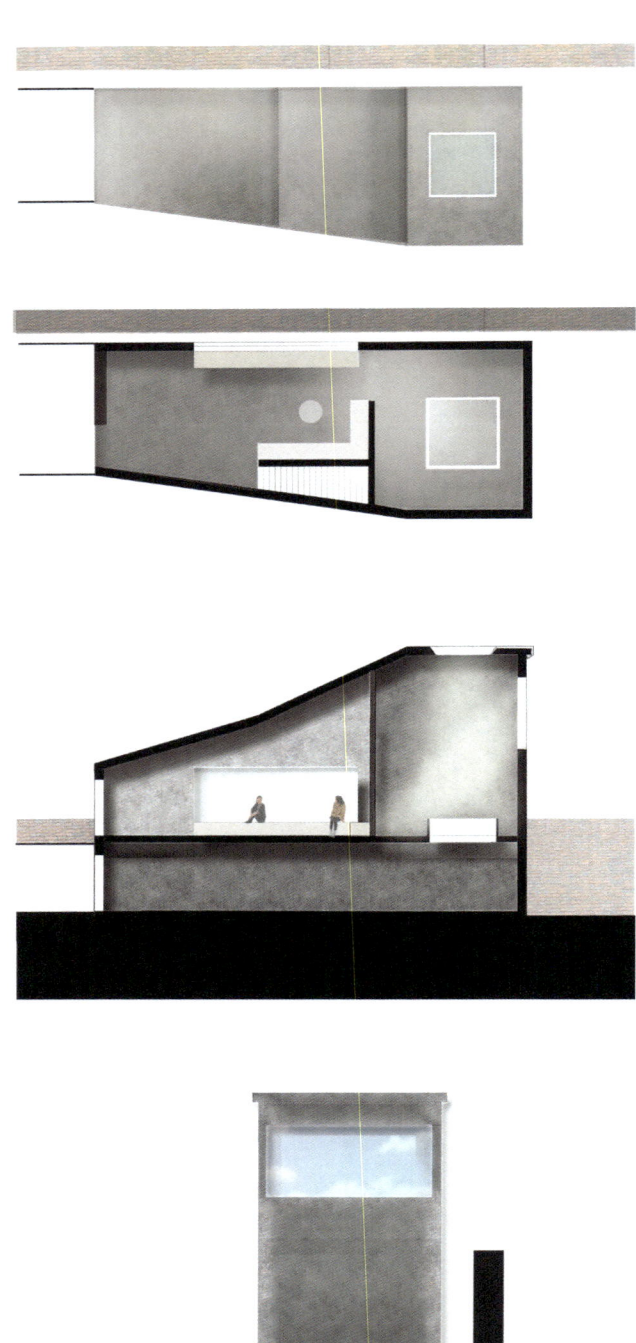

UP: Mirador's night view
LEFT: Elevations and sections of the mirador

The Mirador.

At the end of the journey along the walkway across the wall, there is a Mirador. This Mirador specifically framed views that faces Murano and Burano, showcasing the expansive horizon of Venice.

The Hub:

The creative hub provides facilities for entrepreneurs and students to study, work and to share ideas. Lower ground is a culinary space for workshops to be held for local park-goers to use.

Restaurant:

To cater for the visitors for Castello connections. We have facilitated a dining area that looks below into the restaurant kitchen as well as the views around.

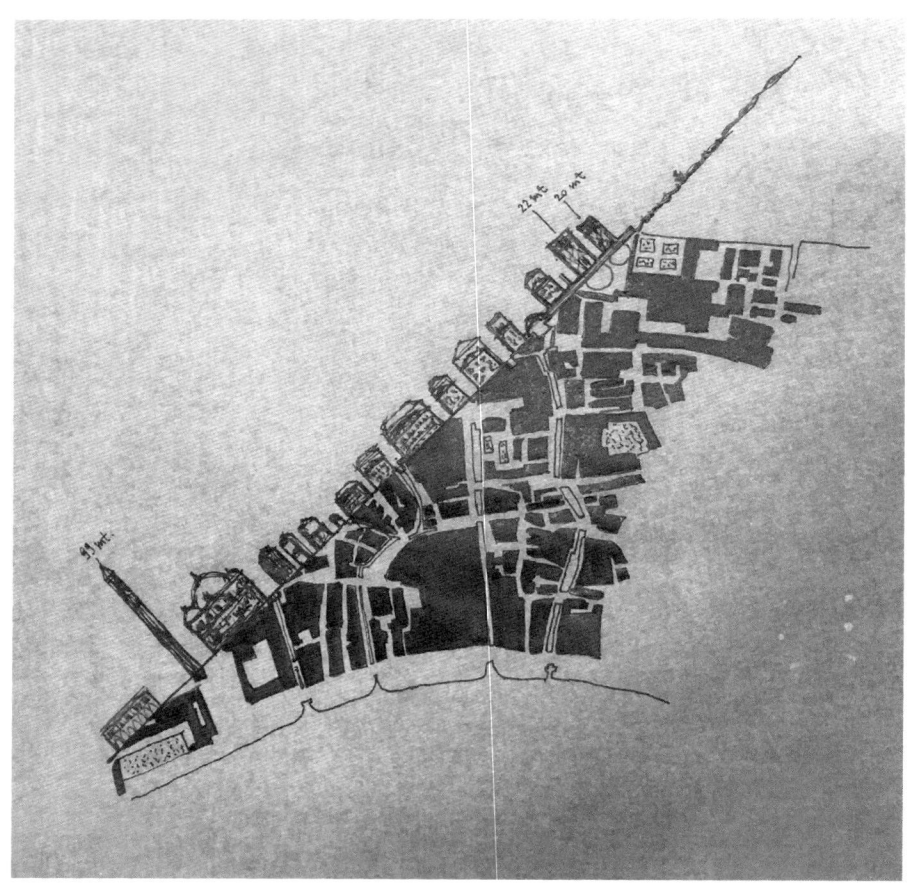

VENICE'S BORDERS adopted clear design principles derived from an in-depth reading of Venice's urban system and Harry Seidler's design principles, while being exposed to the Biennale of Art and Architecture. As a modernist architect, Seidler sought out successful architects, artists, planners, landscape architects and engineers for inspiration and collaboration. Based on Seidler's words "...the essence of modern architecture is based on a coherent ideology embracing and fusing visual and spatial imagination, technological integration and constructional logic.", this studio promoted interdisciplinary learning and a multidisciplinary approach to design.

CONTRIBUTORS

PAOLA FAVARO is a senior lecturer in Architecture in the Faculty of Built Environment at UNSW Sydney. She is a graduate of the IUAV University of Venice and she holds a PhD in Architecture from UNSW. Her research and publications are related to architecture as urban response to the design problems of the contemporary 21st century city. She has written numerous book chapters and papers on Australian architecture and urbanism. She contributed to the Seidler International Symposium (2014), Utzon International Symposium (2014) and she was a key-note speaker with Architect Greg Holman from Harry Seidler & Associates at the ctbuh International Conference Connecting the City (2017) presenting Harry Seidler's Sydney Towers.

ENRICO FONTANARI is Urban Planner, professor of Urban and Landscape Design and Planning in the Department of Architecture and Arts of the IUAV University of Venice, Italy (IUAV).
Chairholder of the Unesco Chair on "Heritage and Urban Regeneration" of the IUAV. Professor in several international post-graduate programs and Director of the Post-graduate Master in "Landscape and Garden Design" of the IUAV. 38 years of international experience in Urban Design and Planning. Is author of various publications on Urban and Landscape Theory and Design and Heritage Preservation.

ANNA-PAOLA POLA is Architect and PhD in Urban Planning. She studied in Venice, Delft and Milan. At the moment she is Director Urban Planner and Research Fellow at WHITRAP, the World Heritage Institute of Training and Research in the Asia-Pacific Region under the auspicies of UNESCO, based at Tongji University in Shanghai. Her main research interests are in urban preservation and sustainable development, with a particular focus on China's small settlements. She curated the Extra-European section of the exhibition "Exporting the Historic Urban Core" for the Triennale di Milano (2015) and is a member of the editorial board of The Journal of Built Heritage (Shanghai).

VALENTINA TRIDELLO is Architect and Assistant Lecturer. She is a graduate of the IUAV University of Venice and the Pontificia Universidad Católica de Chile. Currently enrolled in the European Postgraduate Master in Urbanism (EMU), in collaboration with TU Delft University, KU Leuven, IUAV and UPC in Barcelona. Her major recent contributions accredit multidisciplinary investigations concerning urbanism and social sciences, conducting lectures in developing economies in Latin America, as also leading support to international master courses at the IUAV.

Venice's borders re-interpreted
Seidler International Venice Studio
WORKSHOP

Edited by
Paola Favaro, Anna-Paola Pola
and Valentina Tridello

Editorial Director
Alessandro Franceschini

Published by
LISt Lab
info@listlab.eu
listlab.eu

Art Director & Production
Blacklist Creative, BCN
blacklist-creative.com

ISBN 9788899854690

Printed and bound in the European Union
November 2017

Prohibited total or partial reproduction of this book by any means, without permission of the author and Publisher.

All rights reserved
© of LISt Lab edition;
© of the author's texts;
© of the author's images;

BABEL collection

Promotion and distribution
Messaggerie Libri, Spa, Milano,
Numero verde 800.804.900
assistenza.ordini@meli.it;

International promotion and distribution
ACC Book Distribution Ltd
Woodbridge, Suffolk, IP12 4SD, UK
sales@antique-acc.com

The Scientific Committee of the issues List
Eve Blau (Harvard GSD), Maurizio Carta (University of Palermo), Eva Castro (Architectural Association London) Alberto Clementi (University of Chieti), Alberto Cecchetto (University of Venezia), Stefano De Martino (University of Innsbruck), Corrado Diamantini (University of Trento), Antonio De Rossi (University of Torino), Franco Farinelli (University of Bologna), Carlo Gasparrini (University of Napoli), Manuel Gausa (University of Genova), Giovanni Maciocco (University of Sassari/Alghero), Antonio Paris (University of Roma), Mosè Ricci (University of Trento), Roger Riewe (University of Graz), Pino Scaglione (University of Trento), Claudia Battaino (University di Trento), Luca Zecchin (University di Trento).

LISt Lab is an editorial workshop, based in Europe, that works on contemporary issues. LISt Lab not only publishes, but also researches, proposes, promotes, produces, creates networks.

LISt Lab is a green company committed to respect the environment. Paper, ink, glues and all processings come from short supply chains and aim at limiting pollution. The print run of books and magazines is based on consumption patterns, thus preventing waste of paper and surpluses. LISt Lab aims at the responsibility of the authors and markets, towards the knowledge of a new publishing culture based on resource management.

Built Environment

Università Iuav
di Venezia